To my husband, who embraces every wild idea with love and patience. Thank you for always being ready for the next adventure, no matter how crazy it may seem.

To my daughter Jorian, who has grown into a remarkable woman and is now an essential part of running our companies. I'm endlessly proud of the leader you've become.

To my son, whose decision to serve our country by joining the Air Force fills me with immense pride. Your courage and dedication inspire me every day.

To my parents, for allowing me to explore my imagination and supporting my every dream, no matter how unconventional. Thank you for telling me I could achieve anything I set my mind to—you were right.

To Staci, who came into my life as an assistant and has become an irreplaceable part of this journey. Your dedication, insight, and hard work have made all the difference.

This book is for all of you and for everyone who dares to chase their dreams, navigate the chaos, and rise with grit and grace.

A SPRITZ OF SALES

NAVIGATING ENTREPRENEURSHIP
With **GRIT AND GRACE**

JESSI PARK

Copyright © 2025 by **Jessi Park**

All rights reserved. No part of this book may be reproduced, distributed, or transmitted in any form or by any means, including photocopying, recording, or other electronic or mechanical methods, without the prior written permission of the publisher or author, except in the case of brief quotations embodied in critical reviews and certain other noncommercial uses permitted by copyright law.

ISBN: 978-1-956464-56-6

First Edition 2025

This publication is intended to provide accurate information on the subject matter covered. It is sold with the understanding that neither the author nor the publisher offers legal, investment, accounting, medical, or other professional advice. The author and publisher make no representations or warranties regarding the accuracy or completeness of the contents and expressly disclaim any implied warranties of merchantability or fitness for a particular purpose. No warranties may be extended by sales representatives or materials. Professional consultation is recommended as individual circumstances vary. Neither the author nor the publisher shall be liable for any damages, including but not limited to loss of profit, incidental, or consequential damages.

All rights reserved. Published in the United States by 1973.

TABLE OF CONTENTS

INTRODUCTION, vii

CHAPTER ONE: **START WITH AN IDEA**, 1
    Baggage and Better Options, 3
    The Fragrant Fields, 5
    The Right Idea, 7
    Support Your Ideas with Research, 9
    Take the Leap and the Payback Follows, 13

CHAPTER TWO: **SCENT OF SUCCESS**, 15
    Sales Script, 17
    A Work in Progress, 23

CHAPTER THREE: **MINDSET MATTERS**, 27
    Imposter Syndrome, 32
    The Best Way to "Win" is to Overcome, 34

CHAPTER FOUR: **FIGURE OUT YOUR FINANCES**, 37
    Break in Your Budget, 39
    Cash-In and Cash-Flow, 41
    The Weight of Taxes, 43
    The Finance Defense, 45
    Commit to the Finances, 46

CHAPTER FIVE: **THE BASICS OF YOUR BRAND**, 49
    The Steps, 50
    Put It into Practice, 51
        Logo, 53
        Managing an Online Presence, 54
    Ideal Customer, 55
    Conclusion, 60

CHAPTER SIX: MAKE THE MOST OF YOUR MARKETING, 63
    Understanding the Basics, 65
    The Advanced Elevator Pitch, 67
    The Personal or Professional Approach, 70
    Make the Most of Your Marketing, 73

CHAPTER SEVEN: YOUR #1 TOOL: SOCIAL MEDIA, 75
    Take It Online, 76

CHAPTER EIGHT: YOUR NEW BEST FRIEND, AI, 87
    Ask a Bot, 88
    A Snapshot in Technology, 90
    Communication Rollout, 92
    Look for the Assist, 94

CHAPTER NINE: MANAGING THE HUSTLE, 97
    Time Management, 98
    Your "Second Shift," 100
    The Sacrifice for Success, 101
    Self-Education vs. Education as Procrastination, 103
    Your 24 Hours, 105

CHAPTER TEN: NURTURE AN ENDURING CULTURE, 107
    Quality Culture, 108
    Who's on Your Roster?, 109
    Quality Assurance, 113

CONCLUSION, 115
GLOSSARY, 119
REFERENCES, 127
RECOMMENDED RESOURCES, 129
ACKNOWLEDGMENTS, 135
ABOUT THE AUTHOR, 137

INTRODUCTION

Jenni and I sat on the bed as she opened her presents on her last birthday. It was January 19th, 2021. The guests had long since left; I would soon be sleeping in some corner of this little brownstone. The day had left us both drained, but for different reasons, and had settled into the still of night, and, at least for a little bit, it was just Jenni and me.

She took a little box out of a gift bag and smiled in delight. It was one of her favorites: Sungari perfume from Maurices, the nice department store in Lawrenceville. The square-capped bottle, simple but elegant, had a fresh and clean scent, something to brighten the wearer. Jenni spritzed a little on her small wrists and brought them to her nose. Her face briefly melted into pure delight.

"Oh, I can smell the jasmine."

In such a dark time, Jenni and I shared this little moment of happiness, a brief respite from all the pain she was enduring. She sprayed it everywhere, and the room filled with the bright floral accord, such a sweet smell in such a bitter time. Though I had been living in Orlando for years and Jenni stayed in our small hometown in Illinois, our sisterly bond was unbreakable. We kept up with each other's busy lives mostly through Facebook and phone calls. I could always hear the pride in her voice when she talked about her two children, Evan and Elysia.

Based on her messages and the happy pictures she posted on Facebook, it seemed like she was thriving. At least, until I got a call from our dad in June of 2020.

"Jessi, you really should come up here," he told me. "Jenni isn't doing so well."

"What do you mean?" I asked.

That's when the terrible truth came out: Jenni's cancer, which she had been diagnosed with in August 2019, had spread, and the treatment wasn't working as planned. Everything she had shared on social media and with me personally made things seem fine—she had even been given a bright outlook from her doctors. But Dad's tone told me that may not be the case. I had to get up there as soon as possible. I remember I hopped in the car early that next morning and drove up there as fast as I could, my two kids in tow.

Seeing someone so young fight so hard is unbearably tragic—something that is almost impossible to understand unless you've seen it yourself. And when I saw Jenni, I was shocked. Cancer had ravaged her body. She was all of 90 pounds but refused to speak of her dying. She was a fighter, and she was going to make it.

Having that conversation, broaching that *what-if* with her, was difficult. She did not want to even speak of her dying, and if you brought up talking about any of that, she would get a stern voice and say she was going to be fine.

Jenni was my little sister, after all. I had promised to watch out for her since she came into this world, and that promise still held now. During my visit, I tried to see if there was anything I could do to make things any easier. She just wanted to hang out, so she did my daughter's makeup, and we danced and sang karaoke—one of her favorite things to do.

"You know, I've really been wanting this perfume," she mentioned while I was visiting that July, "but it's just too expensive."

"Really? What is it?"

She told me: Pretty in Purple by Juicy Couture. A hyper-feminine, luxurious scent with a note of jasmine. Jenni always had the best taste. I went online when I got home and ordered her the perfume, plus a bag and glittery gold eyeshadow. (She told me gold brought out the yellow flecks in her blue eyes.) A few days later, she called me.

"Jessi, they sent duplicates! There's two of each," she told me. "You take the other set."

So Jenni and I had matching perfumes, bags, and glitter eyeshadow. Wearing that scent made me feel connected to Jenni from hundreds of miles away. Every time I smelled that middle note of jasmine, I thought of her.

In November of 2020, she was given the all-clear. She was in remission! We talked about how, when she was back to normal, we would go out on the town strutting our matching purses, both wearing our gold eyeshadow and smelling sexy with our Juicy Couture Pretty in Purple. However, in January of 2021, just a few months later, I received the phone call that she had to have emergency surgery due to a bowel blockage. When they went to perform the surgery, they found that the cancer had spread. She was put on hospice immediately. That call shattered my world.

Again, I drove up there immediately. All I wanted to do was spend time with her. I remember getting there just as everyone was singing "Happy Birthday." I rushed through the door and was able to chime in at the last verse. All of her friends and our family were there.

Now, on Jenni's last birthday, there it was again: perfume. Her friend Jessica had gotten it for her at Maurices. In spite of everything, that small luxury lifted her spirits, if only for a moment. Those little things—perfume, lotions, makeup, a nice piece of jewelry—can do so much for a woman.

In one of our very last conversations, I promised Jenni that her two kids, her love and light in this world, would be taken care of. They would always have a roof over their heads, food in their bellies, and a bright future ahead of them. I promised her I'd take them on trips in the summer and for back-to-school shopping. I could not fix the situation we were in, but I at least had the resources to make good on my final promise to my sister.

My sister, Jennifer Elysia Park Bossenberry, passed away on January 31st, 2021. Though she is no longer with us, her legacy carries on in her beautiful children, my niece and nephew. But soon after her passing, I had an idea for another kind of legacy: to create a company inspired by our mutual love of perfume and in honor of my sister—a company that could one day offer employment and/or partial ownership to my niece and nephew, if they wanted. Thus, Elysian Parfum was born.

The name turned out to be a bit of a God wink—I chose the name because it incorporated my niece's and nephew's first names but later learned that Elysian means "relating to or characteristic of heaven or paradise." The name had Jenni all over it, and I didn't even know it.

Elysian Parfum first gained traction online for our on-the-nose "dupes" of other perfumes, but I've since taught myself the art and science of perfumery and focus solely on original creations now. It has taken on a life of its own as I study and create this brand from scratch, maybe slightly obsessed. However, I really want it to be something she would be proud of. I wanted to create a little touch of luxury for everyone so they could be transformed the same way Jenni did when she sprayed Pretty in Purple and Sungari. This brand embodied a vision of chic, delicious scents for men *and* women. It's been amazing to see the response we've gotten from our customers.

I didn't have any background in e-commerce, retail, or perfume. Not only did I launch Elysian Parfum, but I also started my own bag line called Execuluxe®. Was it a risk? Heck yes! But I felt in my bones that this would be a success. I'd only ever sold an intangible—albeit highly necessary—product before: insurance. I started Elysian Parfum and Execuluxe® with no significant knowledge of manufacturing or production. I had nothing but an idea in my mind and a love for perfume and bags, and that was it.

But I *am* an entrepreneur, and I've always had the determination to do anything I put my mind to. I'd gone from a single mother on unemployment benefits and food stamps to the founder and president of Inspired Insurance Solutions, LLC, and I did it with the will to learn and the mindset to make it happen. If I could accomplish that, then I knew I could do this. I just had to.

In the past few years, I've launched two cruelty-free luxury brands: Elysian Parfum and Execuluxe®, a patent-pending line of traveling bags for professional women. Before that, I worked my way up to becoming a multimillion-dollar producer in the insurance world and founded my very own agency. And before that, I became an internationally-collected artist. I accomplished all of this while raising my two children on my own.

The point of running through my resume is to tell you that, while yes, it was a *tough* road to take, I did it—and you can do it too. Anyone can become an entrepreneur, and anyone can succeed at it. You just need the dedication, the discipline, and sometimes a little nudge in the right direction. That is what *A Spritz of Sales* (hopefully) is.

This book is not the end-all, be-all guide to entrepreneurship. I'm not peddling any get-rich-quick schemes. It takes blood, sweat, and tears, and, above all, *time* to build a successful and sustainable business. If you aren't willing to put in the time and effort to make it happen, you're better off setting this book back on the shelf right now.

I am not going to sit here and try to claim to be the foremost expert either. But I have my own experience, my ups-and-downs of this journey, and lessons learned along the way, which I'll be sharing with you as honestly as possible. There's no gatekeeping here—I'll tell you exactly how I've done it and include specific resources that you can access online.

Entrepreneurship is for everyone, and I'll share what I know to get you off the ground.

CHAPTER ONE
START WITH AN IDEA

There are probably millions of books, videos, courses, articles, and podcasts on starting a business. They all (hopefully) have their own unique approach, but many prescribe the same foundational advice: identify a market gap, find a profitable product to fill it, and sell the hell out of it. *Boom*. It doesn't matter if it's dog treats or discount eyewear—it's about the numbers, and if the margins are high and the costs are low, then you better start hawking whatever that thing may be. That's Business 101, and that's exactly what you should do.

And that's exactly what I didn't.

Instead of starting with something that sells, I started with an idea. I didn't go with what seemed like the surest path to profit; instead, I went with what I was passionate about and genuinely wanted to see out in the world. Despite what many people might tell you, the insurance world isn't a place where money rains on even the worst agents. It is a ruthless industry full of cutthroat agents, cold calls, and uncertainty. It's no surprise that the overwhelming majority of agents will fail to establish a career. The failure rate of a new agent is as high as 92 percent. *92 percent.* And even knowing all that, I still turned down a comfortable job in marketing to pursue insurance. The question is obvious—*Why would you make such a gamble like that?*—and the answer is just as simple: *Because I loved it.*

Of course, I don't necessarily mean the ins and outs of insurance itself, but I loved getting to help people. I *loved* getting on that phone and working with everyone from Debby in Louisiana to Dan in Indiana to create a full coverage plan for them and their families. Bringing this kind of peace and protection to people was what made me dial in every single day. I loved the thought that every policy I sold took me closer to my dream of financial freedom and residual income. The joy and satisfaction I got from a job well done carried me through all the toughest times, the many sleep-starved nights spent on the phone, all the way to creating Inspired Insurance Solutions. If I had taken the marketing job instead, I don't think I would have gone nearly as far with it as I have in insurance—at least not like this. I also wouldn't know the freedom of being self-employed and an employer, rather than an employee.

This passion is the same reason I launched Execuluxe® and Elysian Parfum instead of just selling, say, fishing tackles. I'm sure there's some outdoorsman out in the world who would love to start a business like that, but I personally don't care about fishing tackles *at all*. I don't even fish! But I do care about having chic traveling bags for professionals and delectable perfume and cologne that would make my sister proud. I am proud of every product I've brought to market, and it's my dedicated passion that sustains me through all the hardships it takes to "make it." When you care about what you're doing, you don't quit—not until you've succeeded or seen it through. No matter what your business is about, it has to start from a place of passion. It's the only path to a truly successful (and yes, profitable) business.

Baggage and Better Options

I knew I had hit a major milestone in my insurance career when I was invited to join the 8% Nation Tour. Traveling to multiple cities in a matter of months, I would be speaking to large audiences about my success in insurance and offering advice for them to achieve the same wins. Being offered such a large platform in this way was a huge affirmation of everything I had accomplished in insurance at this point—after all, the "8%" refers to the 8 percent of insurance producers who achieve this level of success in the industry.

Suffice to say, this was a *big* deal, and as such, I prepared for it. When I boarded my first of many flights for the tour, I knew I was accomplished, well-informed, and had polished attire. Despite all my experience and preparation, there was one snag: my belongings. I was constantly juggling my phone, important documents, sometimes my computer, and always a cup of coffee. Imagine trying to shake hands with that load in the way!

I soon noticed that this was much more of a "woman problem." Men had sleek bags and numerous pockets to carry their things in. While there are briefcases available, I searched high and low for a functional, feminine bag that would suit my business needs without compromising my style. I didn't want some clunky rolling bag trailing behind me like an Avon lady—I wanted a purse so expansive that it could carry my work, snacks, *and* personal effects while still being a fashionable part of my ensemble. There was nothing on the market, and I knew that if I really wanted a bag like that, I'd have to make it myself.

Now, I'm not a craftsman. I haven't worked with fabrics or leather; however, I *do* know how to hunt down resources. After some Googling, I found Pietra, the supplier platform. Pietra lets you connect with manufacturers and select them based on your needs. Some will only offer a minimum batch of 10k, while others are more willing to work with small businesses. It can be a daunting task to stare down a manufacturing directory. You can also utilize websites like ImportYeti.com to find out where other companies in your field import their supplies and inventory. What does your idea require to be successful? Make that list and see which suppliers align with it.

By working with manufacturers and having custom elements designed, I was able to create my patented, vegan, and cruelty-free Execuluxe®. Execuluxe® isn't your awkward rolling backpack or Avon ensemble; it's a chic and sleek traveling bag that lets you glide through airports and conference rooms without worry. And they are *sexy*, really. One of my favorite bags has a black crocodile-esque material on the outside and a red lining on the inside, just like the famed Louboutin shoes.

On Louboutins—something I've heard other women say all too often is, "When you buy a pair of Loubs, expect to suffer." When it comes to designer shoes and bags, pinched toes and pitiful storage space are all part of the territory. It's fashion after all; beauty is pain. Famous brands aren't thinking about the logistics for their wearers. They don't have to. People will buy their product either way.

But Execuluxe®? I thought every last detail out. As a bag girl, I have so many pieces in my collection that are *almost* perfect: a cute tote with bad straps, a purse with barely enough space to put my phone, little oversights that forced me to compromise fashion over function. When it came to my own collection, I simply refused to make that tradeoff. Pain and inconvenience are not prerequisites of fashion. I was determined to figure out a way to combine aesthetic and practical details. How could I create versatile, thoughtful, and stylish pieces that held up to the trials and travels of the working woman? My resulting research and product development led to Execuluxe®.

The bags became everything I was looking for, and I knew other women would feel the same way. All the initial work I put in to fulfill my vision empowered me to take that last leap. I ordered that first batch and the rest is history in the making.

The Fragrant Fields

I had already begun my work with the bags when the perfume idea came to me. It was a passion I shared with my sister, and, in the months after her passing, I often found myself thinking of Jenni and wondering, "What would she have wanted?" What would she have wanted for her childrens' futures? I wanted to establish a legacy for my sister, something that they could feel a part of one day. So began my fragrance work.

I had always been a big fragrance head and started reviewing my own perfume stash on the dresser. I have never been fixated on wearing the most expensive, fancy brands you see on billboards. I buy based on what I like, not for any imagined "prestige." I first purchased Bijan's DNA simply because the bottle matched my all-purple vanity, and I will always love Warm Vanilla Sugar by Bath & Body Works. I began by considering what had first attracted me to these perfumes: the labels, the bottles, the scent notes—what drove me to make each purchase? What made these brands so successful? My research was just getting started. I didn't even know about base, middle, and top notes when I began my work. I went from clueless fragrance enthusiast to visiting a Californian perfume academy so I could mix original scents. That trip was a game-changer, elevating me from a passionate apprentice to someone seriously committed to perfumery.

It was there that I created my first custom perfume, complete with 11 scent notes. I think of it as the perfect summer scent—not summery like a strong coconut base, as so many other perfumes are. No, I wanted it to smell like walking through a garden on a Hawaiian island, a light breeze on your skin as the plumerias bloom under moonlight.

Standing in the Californian laboratory, I had the chance to test, smell, and mix as much as I wanted to. The chemist advised me on what scents and profiles blend well together and which don't. I learned about base notes, pre-made accords (already layered scents) and asked questions until the clock ran out. I wrapped up the trip by visiting the Aftel Archive of Curious Scents museum with my son in tow. Perfumer Mandy Aftel only used scents from nature, and the resulting museum looks like a medieval apothecary with dried plants, original bottles, and perfume recipe books dating back to the 1500s. I felt like an alchemist. This trip brought me in contact with a family perfumery legacy I was unknowingly joining by starting Elysian Parfum.

After completing one of those ancestry kits, I traced my lineage all the way back to England on my dad's side and France on my mom's. Her people came from Grasse, France. To the average person, that may seem inconsequential, but with my love of perfume, I saw the significance. Grasse is considered *the* perfume capital of the world. I can't whip out a journal that proves the trade of my ancestors, but I do know they worked in the raw materials trade. And if we're thinking about France in the early 19th century, working with raw materials meant that they either *were* perfumers or worked for them. I never expected that the exploration of perfume would lead to not only a successful e-commerce business but also a personal connection to this enduring trade. The signs are clear: Perfumery might just be in my blood. At the very least, it was a journey I needed to take.

The Right Idea

Don't let the heading fool you—I'm not about to share some groundbreaking idea for you to make bank on. For me, I believe the right idea is one that you're passionate about *with* the chance to add market value. Entrepreneurship will inevitably take time and work; without passion, your journey will become an exhausting grind in pursuit of success.

Many so-called business "gurus" would tell me that I did everything wrong. The entire Execuluxe® line is comprised of high-ticket, bulky items that are hard to store in large quantities and are not readily available to purchase from suppliers, while fragrances already saturate the market with dupes and high-end scents. I didn't approach either business venture with this limiting mindset though. It wasn't a question of what was going to be the easiest thing to sell—it was a question of what I was passionate about and what I would take pride in. I launched products that *I* would want to buy.

That's not to say you should leap at every whim. You do need a stable idea that you can dedicate yourself to while still offering market opportunity. Start with your idea and reflect on the following questions:

- What would you want to buy?
- What could you see other people buying?
- Is there a market for it?

- Can you put in the initial investment required for this product?

Think through these questions and start to create your game plan. Not everything has to be defined and aligned, but I do encourage you to take the time to thoroughly research your ideas and options. Every bit of data can be stored in your arsenal to use later.

Here also is where you should look to the future. Suppose you make a dent in the market—your product gains traction and people start to recognize your brand. Now consider, is your idea scalable? If not, your success is limited before you even start. Doing the appropriate research early can save you from having clipped wings later. Let's say you start off with leggings. What else can you add to that line to make it scalable? Immediately, I think of sports bras, shirts, workout shorts, socks, etc. Those are all potential avenues.

You might think, *So what if my idea isn't scalable? What if I just want to sell one item and only one item? What's wrong with that?* Technically, nothing is *wrong* with just selling a specific type of hair clip or certain kitchen gadget. It's just that you limit your sales to one-time buys from customers you'll likely never see again, and when you limit your sales, you limit your success.

If your entire business is riding on one singular item that may or may not continue to sell after it initially hits the market, it's frankly not a sustainable business idea. Consumer taste can change fast, and if your item was nothing more than a brief trend, you'll find yourself shuttering the metaphorical doors before you even realize what happened. Think of all the people who took the leap to sell fidget spinners, selfie sticks, oversized hair claws, quirky astrology clothes, etc. How many of them do you think are still in business? It doesn't take more than a cursory Google search to find plenty of stories of people who emptied their savings account on the next "big thing," only to fill their garages with stock that won't sell.

You might be asking yourself, *What exactly does she mean by "scalable?"* If you are, don't worry—I'll explain. Scalability simply refers to the structural potential of your company to grow, both as a business and a brand. This means whether you can expand business to new regions, add more products or services to your offerings, capture new markets, and overall build your business on a larger scale (hence the term, *scalability*). To determine if your business has room to grow over time, you will have to conduct thorough research to assess the initial idea as it is now. Luckily, that's what we're talking about next.

Support Your Ideas with Research

Launching your idea takes courage, but you should support your ideas with research. Before you get to beta models and product testing, you need to hop online and see what similar products exist—how can you improve upon the existing market? Maybe this means selling at a lower price point or making a higher quality product. A good number to shoot for is to try to improve or differentiate the product by at least 10 percent. That may mean better features, higher quality materials and packaging, or more accessories. Between Elysian Parfum and Execuluxe®, I took both of these approaches. Don't be afraid of competition because you can still make your mark. Think of how many hundreds of perfume companies exist—and yet, I still run a steady business. You just have to make sure you have a unique twist that embodies your brand.

A critical part of researching is reviewing all of the components of your products, including the cost. The perfume isn't just comprised of the fragrance. I had to examine the sprayers, the caps, the collars, the labels, bottle shape, etc., in addition to the scent formulas. A challenge here was that many suppliers won't work with small businesses. Even with resources like Pietra, you have to be cognisant of the added costs for all of the pieces involved. One specific requirement for my purses and perfume was to ensure they're not tested on animals. The thought of testing on animals was an automatic no—I love all animals and couldn't stomach the idea of them suffering for the sake of fashion or beauty. I also wanted to work with industry standard clean ingredients and try to steer away from excess plastic packaging as much as possible. These are principles that are important to me, and I wanted my brands to reflect that.

After almost a year of development and lots of uncertainty and second-guessing myself, I came to realize that people value everything Execuluxe® and Elysian Parfum have to offer, and they are willing to pay for it. This is ultimately the key. Whatever your business idea may be, you need to ask yourself these three critical questions:

1. **Is there a market for what I am offering, both now and in the future?**

    You need to research whether or not there is an actual need/desire for your idea. If you want to sell diabetic pet treats, Google it and see what comes up. Is this too niche of a concept? How many businesses exist right now? How many orders have they received? Sometimes this is explicitly shown online, sometimes you can gauge this through the number of reviews, and other times you can check Semrush and Spyfu to see how they get their traffic and what ads they are running.

Again, this is also where the question of sustainability and scalability comes in. Will your target demographic (in this case, owners of diabetic pets) need/want this product in the future, or is it a passing fad? How long have your prospective competitors existed? Have they pivoted from one thing to another in that time, or have they been able to sell the same things over time? If they've expanded their offerings, what have they added and what could you potentially add in the future? Each and every one of these questions must be carefully considered.

2. **What is unique about what I am offering that will make people choose my product/service over another one?**

For me, I have a different answer for each one of my businesses. With a patent-pending design that creates space and accommodates every item like a chic professional's luxury version of the Mary Poppins bag, there is literally no other bag quite like Execuluxe® on the market. And while there are plenty of perfumes out there, Elysian Parfum offers niche fragrances using the finest ingredients sourced from all over the world. It is the accessibility, variety, and affordable luxury that makes Elysian Parfum stand out from other brands. Inspired Insurance Solutions, LLC, is one of a countless number of insurance agencies out there, but my agency offers the same value that I bring to every phone call: Each agent at Inspired Insurance Solutions is hired, trained, and empowered to be whip-smart with building plans, personable with their clients, and above all, care about the person on the other end of the line. Our clients come away feeling that their agent has done everything they can to craft the best coverage possible. When have you last felt that after ending a call with your insurance agent?

Each and every one of you will have a unique value proposition, the certain x-factor that makes your product/service stand out in the sea of competitors and places you at the top. If you don't have that, then you're not going to succeed in the long run. Think about what makes your idea different and better than other products or services. What are you bringing to the table? What are you adding to the industry? Why would a customer choose to spend money at your business over anyone else's? It's a brutal self-assessment, but one you must commit to all the same.

3. **Are people willing to pay for it?**

This is the central question that anyone in business will keep coming back to. Some starry-eyed business neophytes believe in the (misquoted) line from both the Old Testament and the 1989 film *Field of Dreams*: "If you build it, they will come." It's a nice concept: If you just believe in yourself and launch the business, it will succeed. It sounds simple—except it's not.

If you build it—and don't perform thorough market research to validate or disprove your idea, educate yourself on the fundamentals of business, and take time to brand your business along the way—people may not come, and you may go bankrupt instead. It takes a lot of learning and reflection to see if a business will work in the first place, and it all starts with the basic question: Will someone buy this?

It's a question that can be answered through research and testing, through reviewing the current market online and conducting polls for your target demographic. The saying goes, "the customer is always right," but people don't seem to really understand the actual significance of it. It doesn't mean that customers have a free license to demand refunds for their finished meal; it means that a business needs to pay attention and pivot to where their customers are putting their money. If you notice that your clothing line is quickly selling out of XL shirts, you should probably stock more of that size and even consider expanding your size offerings. If many of your bakery's customers buy the vegan croissant and leave feedback asking for a vegan version of your cinnamon rolls, you would be a fool not to start baking vegan cinnamon rolls. Money talks, the customer is usually right, and your prospective ones will tell you whether or not your idea is something they'd buy.

Take the Leap and the Payback Follows

No one is going to come to you and tell you when it's time to leap. Once you have your idea and your research in hand, be prepared to take that step. It's scary to venture out into the unknown, and there is no guarantee of success, but you have to have the faith and courage to do it anyway. So, take a breath, stand up tall, and take that first step into the market.

I had carried my sample Execuluxe® around for six months before ordering 10,000 for inventory. It takes painstaking care to achieve a product you can be proud of. Every dollar and hour that I poured into the products was worth it as the sales and positive feedback rolled in. That meant late-night hours rehashing designs and fragrance concepts over and over and studying competitors and trends.

Eventually, I reached a point where I wanted to move. I had lived in Florida most of my life, and it felt like time for a change. While searching for the right change in scenery, I took into account that I would need room for thousands of purses and my perfume-making organ. That led me to a home in North Georgia, where the houses and land came at a fairer price, and you could get so much more bang for your buck.

I never thought that my ideas would take me to a perfumery shop in California or uproot me to Georgia, but in taking that leap and embracing my passion, the businesses came alive. At a certain point, you can only do so much market research and deliberation. You will have to take your own leap of faith and commit to your idea—whether that means time, energy, money, taking a course to learn more, etc. It's going to take some level of sacrifice, and if you're hungry for it, the following success will make it all worthwhile.

When I started my insurance career, I had many less-than-restful nights toiling away to get everything done. But you have to give up a little bit of your current life to cultivate the life you really want. Now, with both companies running simultaneously, I'm back in that same situation, doing the work every day. Sometimes I'm pouring over research until the early morning or waking up to pack products before my insurance work, but it's all worthwhile. This is the life of an entrepreneur. It's about building something for the future—for your children, grandchildren, and beyond.

SCENT OF SUCCESS

When you close your eyes and think of the words "success in business," a certain popular image might pop into your head: that confident man in a tailored suit stepping out of a sports car, on his way to make another million. This entrepreneur is focused, he's sharp, and he's aggressive. He will do what it takes to succeed, and he will not stop until he does. It's a formidable image—and a little off-putting. Not everyone wants to be *that* guy in business, and the good news is, you don't have to be.

The insurance world is famous for its pushy salesmen, harassing prospects over policies until they get the "yes." This is an aggressive approach to cold calling, and it didn't take me long to realize that I was not going to address my clients this way. In fact, I did not last very long at the first insurance agency—a captive agency—because I couldn't align myself with their values. They had a full *Wolf of Wall Street* mentality, using harsh sales tactics (not to mention hard drugs in the office) to close deals at all costs. They even pushed agents to hang up on clients if they had any pre-existing conditions like diabetes. I'm no "guru," and I don't belong on some sort of pedestal or anything, but I knew that the insurance world could be different. As you build your business, you may feel pressured to adopt the existing cutthroat mentality, or you might focus solely on efficiency and the bottom line. But it's your personal touch that can really make your business a success, making you both memorable and irreplaceable.

Yes, I still had to cold call to build up my client book—that's unavoidable—but instead of rattling off those calls, I took the time to really *listen* and hear the concerns prospects brought up. I ignored the slimy ABC (Always Be Closing) script where every line is a sales pitch. Instead, I had a radical idea: I treated them like the humans they are. Humans who, like everyone else, have wants, needs, and fears. It became my job to see these people and fulfill their needs rather than seeing them as cash cows on my way to prosperity. Competitors would maybe call this a too-soft, "sell like a girl" perspective, but the numbers don't lie—I've surpassed $150 million in sales, and my business shows no signs of slowing down. This isn't a humble brag; it's the reality of having a game-changing approach to a familiar industry. Your business may be in a saturated market, but if you offer something new, whether that's a product or service or the way you approach it, you can create a distinguished brand that buoys you to success. Early in my endeavor, it was obvious that prospects responded to my realness. I quickly gained clients, and they gifted me their trust. I didn't play the numbers or manipulate anyone. Instead, I created Inspired Insurance Solutions using a basic recipe for success. I combined my carefully cultivated insurance knowledge with the inherent qualities that set me apart.

Beyond the skills for the job at hand, you'll need a:
- pint of work ethic,
- heaping cup full of setting your intentions,
- quarter cup of people skills,

- dash of luck, and
- pinch of being a badass (and not giving up when it gets tough).

There's no one avenue for success. It comes down to the qualities, mindset, and intention with which you pursue your goals.

If you're just starting out with your business, you're in a delicate stage of growth. Whether you're selling the product to consumers, pitching the company to potential employees in the hopes of acquiring their skills, or selling to prospective investors, you need to iron out your sales script.

Sales Script

To craft your sales script, you need to first understand the principles of sales. The principles of sales isn't some long-winded theory or an overly obvious acronym like Always Be Closing. It's actually quite simple: Treat people like, *well*, people, and talk to them accordingly. If you went to a local car dealership, would you prefer to be accosted and pushed by someone only looking for their commission, or would you prefer to have a no-pressure conversation with someone who is most interested in helping you choose the best vehicle? The answer should be obvious. Who, then, do you think ultimately closes more sales? It's not hard to imagine that for all the movies and online courses extolling the success of the relentless salesperson, the one who is more genuine and respectful is going to come out on top over time.

Yes, you are ultimately looking to make a sale from your potential clients and customers, but they are more than just their dollars. Remember every single time you've been on the other end of a sale, and let that inform your approach. Recognize their humanity, and they will respond in kind.

Whatever your product or service, selling it without coming across as a heartless salesman is a nuanced art. From my years in insurance, I've learned that people respond best to other people. It may sound obvious, but think about the last time you heard, "I'm calling about your car's extended warranty." It sounded kind of mechanical, even if it was a real person on the other line, right? You can hear the tired repetition in the phrasing alone, nevermind the somewhat bored voice reciting it.

That's why I have a fresh conversation every time. Yes, there are basic steps to follow, but I inject humanity into my sales scripts in order to become someone who my clients can talk to and trust. My sales script is a loose line of questions that flows through the major touchpoints I need for a client's policies while still having the natural rhythm of conversation. Now, this script is written specifically for my insurance work; however, it can easily be adapted across all industries. You need to establish a natural engagement while demonstrating a confident mastery of whatever it is you are selling.

I always start with an opener. Arguably, it's the most important part of the sale. Remember, you have about seven seconds to make an impression. I need to be quick, to the point, and engaging. I need to make sure my voice has some pep in it. With that, I always make sure I end the sentence with an open-ended question. This builds rapport, makes them think on their toes, and usually sets the stage for a quality conversation to follow. For this example, let's say you are the proud owner-operator of Nicole's Nice Soaps and have a table at the farmer's market. This could be more or less how you open a conversation with anyone who comes over to look at your wares:

Opener: *Hi, I'm Nicole! Please feel free to pick up anything you'd like and ask me any questions about my soaps. What's your name, by the way?*

Next, you want to qualify yourself and build that sense of trust in your ability to help them. What makes you different from the dozens of other vendors they've walked by today? Use this to talk yourself up. Have you gotten any sort of recognition? Have you been in business for a certain number of years? This is where you can talk about what makes you stand apart from your competition. Make it clear that this isn't a sales pitch but rather the start of a long-term, mutually beneficial relationship.

Qualification: *That soap you picked up is made with locally-sourced goat's milk and lavender from my backyard. I've been creating sustainable soaps for the last ten years, and the lavender scent sells out every weekend I come out here.*

Now I take out my **Intake Form** or Questionnaire. Be personable as you go through the questions. Don't make it seem like a sterile quiz; talk to them while you do it.

Questions/Intake Form: *Do you have any skin concerns you'd like to address or any preferences?*

Use this section to relate to the person no matter what you sell. If you sell windows, then start asking them all of the questions that you need to know in order for you to address their inquiry or fix the problem they are having. Do this in a conversational manner, working through each question with them.

Next is the budgeting question. Be aware that this can be a sensitive topic, so be sure to speak with empathy. This is important because you want to know if the client you are about to diligently comb through quotes for has a reasonable budget or if you need to reset their expectations.

Again, let's use windows as an example. Keep in mind, I don't know anything about windows, but I imagine an intake form would have questions on it relating to the different thickness of glass, the trim options, and the different types of windows that are available. As you go through and ask them their preference on each of these, be prepared to explain each detail to let them know what they have an option of. With an item as simple as soaps, this might not be as detailed and may look like the example below.

Budgeting: *Are you looking to just get one today, or are you interested in my "buy three, get one free" deal?*

Finally, you need to reassure them. Ideally, you will get right to work with your client and offer a few options that would meet their needs. For people in other businesses, this could look like a final rundown of their order as well as some sort of guarantee on delivery and quality service. However you need to proceed, a simple reassurance goes a long way. Let them know that you are there for them, you can be reached after the sale, and reiterate what makes you stand out from your competition.

A big factor when I sold was making people feel like they were in charge. This is essentially true—we went with whatever option we picked out together. I made commission no matter what they chose, so I wanted to help them find the best plan for their needs. Giving them the option to tell you what they don't like or building options for them reduces the "salesy" feeling, and they begin to look at you like a partner.

Reassure Them: *Okay, awesome! I'm so excited you're going for the bundle. I'm going to pick out a few scents similar to the lavender one, and I might be able to help with skin dryness for when you go up north next week, but you let me know which ones you want and I'll pack them up for you. Whatever you choose, I just know you're going to love them.*

Throughout your conversation, be sure to continue with the open-ended questions and really get to know your clients. Also, *during* your conversation, you should be trying to find their **pain point**. A pain point is a person's central issue, often driven by their wants, needs, or fears. The pain point is what you need to address with the right product or solutions. Be sure to occasionally repeat their pain point back to them as you present the options. This is also how you will find areas where you can add value for your client.

I wrote this sales script based on what *I* would want to hear from a professional. And, if I was being sold insurance, I would like to buy it from a *person*, someone who is keeping my best interests in mind. You have to keep in mind that, as large companies get bigger and AI gets smarter, we will really need to rely on our "humanness" to connect with people. Most people don't enjoy phoning call centers and getting transferred five times to different customer service representatives. They want to talk to someone they like, know, and trust. So use this to your advantage as you build your clientele.

If you can ask your potential client the questions on a person-to-person level rather than robotically going through a list, then you'll be able to build rapport with them and establish the trust needed to make the sale. Another aspect of this open dialogue might not be as "teachable," and that's empathy. Lean into these qualities, especially the ones that are dismissed as "weak." Those are often the personality traits that will set you apart from the rest of the crowd. This is also where I often see women excel in sales—empathy is a quality that usually comes easily to women. While some would dismiss kindness and understanding as weakness with sales, these are actually attributes that can help you create a loyal customer base (and committed employees).

This next crucial skill is something I learned at my very first job. Back then, all McDonald's employees were required to give all customers the option to "super-size" their meal. So for about 40 cents extra, you could get a larger fry and drink. It's quite genius; it's a few extra fries and about a cup of extra soda, which is essentially water, multiplied by billions of customers. But I didn't want to be another voice droning, "Would you like to supersize that?"

I was really uncomfortable asking customers to buy more. It felt so "salesy" to me. I ended up getting written up twice for not doing it. My manager at the time threatened to outright fire me if I ever got caught not offering the super-size option. So I had to change my approach and started asking every customer if they wanted to super-size their meal, but with my own dash of personality added to the "pitch." It's not too hard to sell food to someone who's already waited in that drive-through line, but you can still adapt and incorporate that relaxed tone in order to "sell like a girl" and reach new business heights.

A Work in Progress

There's always going to be people out there saying you're doing your work wrong. But you wouldn't be an entrepreneur if you let doubt get in the way of your success. Yes, you'll make the wrong decision at times—that's a natural part of the process. I like to think of my business (and myself) as a continual work in progress. After all, if you're scoring tens across the board, where is the motivation to try harder and be better? Every day offers the chance to improve upon the day before.

My entry into insurance was absolutely a work in progress. I didn't step into a career with full benefits, a six-figure salary, and comfortable working hours. In fact, when I first ventured into the insurance world, my morale was at an all time low. Insurance, with a paycheck based on commission, was a risk. After a few months of really struggling, I saw the massive potential in insurance and residual income, and I knew that I had to at least try. And once I put my mind to something, I move forward with full force and dedication. I *was* going to do this. I held onto my confidence in the products and in my skills to get it out there.

Despite my years as an entrepreneur, e-commerce has also brought challenges for me to overcome. Much like my own products, my e-commerce knowledge is a work in progress. I'm not an expert or a self-proclaimed guru—I'm a woman on a mission to turn my ideas into successful, sustainable businesses.

This book is a memento to my continual education in building businesses. I've made mistakes, but I've learned from them. And tomorrow, I may make another mistake. But that's the beauty of business-building: There's always a puzzle to solve and work to do. The moment you become complacent, you've lost.

My book is not the definitive or complete guide to success. I've found success by persevering and adapting my model. I can't promise all of your business questions will be answered here, but I can provide transparency. I'll share my stories, I'll pass along some of my favorite resources, and I'll take you along the path I've walked so you can incorporate it into your own journey.

Entrepreneurialism is not a get-rich-quick scheme, so if you're looking for an easy route, this isn't for you. If you're looking to build a sustainable source of income for you and your family, you have to do it right, and there are simply no shortcuts here. You have to work, adapt, and persist.

There's one thing I've always wished for, and it's that I wish I had known about the insurance industry when I was younger. Much of a person's success in their 20s has to do with who their parents are. By that, I mean that if your parents are poor, you're not going to have the connections necessary to present your ideas and network, the safety net to take big risks and potentially fail, or the opportunity to accept unpaid internships knowing that your bills will be covered by your parents. Rags to riches stories are extremely rare, especially in this day and age. But entrepreneurship, especially using insurance as a vehicle, is a definite opportunity. Success doesn't happen overnight, no matter how good your ideas are. You have to sacrifice to build your company from the ground up, but the beauty of business is that *anyone can do it*. Of course, this is only true if you're willing to do the work. I worked myself up from the bottom to become a successful insurance agent to the founder of Inspired Insurance Solutions and my two e-commerce businesses, Elysian Parfum and Execuluxe®.

These businesses are my ultimate passions. That doesn't mean I was instantly successful. I've had to "hack" the work and use my skills. I've had to go through really difficult hardships and work from the ground up. Pick and choose what works for you and put yourself into high gear to pursue that "unattainable" dream. All you have to do is believe that this was meant for you, come up with an action plan, and get started.

CHAPTER THREE
MINDSET MATTERS

I have spent the past seven years learning the ins and outs of insurance. I've attended over 20 conferences, served hundreds of clients, and built a network of over 200 agents. I don't say this to brag but to demonstrate my credentials. I've worked hard for my success and yet, at every turn, there were people waiting to dismiss my efforts, spreading false rumors about me sleeping my way to success or portraying me as some sort of controlling, power-hungry b*tch. I'll admit, those sort of comments used to hurt. But then I realized that the people making them were jealous, insecure, or a bitter combination of both. Now, I have the strength of mind to laugh off their comments. As a woman in business, it's a harsh reality that you need to grow a thick skin and take the high road. Only by securing the right mindset will you start to enjoy your successes instead of being riddled with doubt.

You need fortitude and a strong moral compass to succeed. Plenty of people pursue a life of entrepreneurship for the money alone. While the payoff for your hard work can be incredibly rewarding, that alone won't sustain you through the challenges that come with running a business.

In order to take your idea from the intangible to a functioning, profitable business, you need to have the skills and mindset of an entrepreneur. Some of these are inherent traits you may already possess, but others you may need to nurture and strengthen. The best entrepreneurs are those who embody these qualities:

- Critical thinking and problem-solving
- Flexibility and adaptability
- Communication and collaboration
- Comfort with risk
- Initiative and self-reliance
- Future orientation
- Opportunity recognition
- Creativity and innovation

Among my key strengths are critical thinking and problem-solving. I largely credit these to my childhood days spent immersed in role-playing games such as Legends of Zelda and Super Mario Brothers. Those games didn't just entertain me; they honed my ability to navigate complex scenarios and sharpened my analytical thinking. Communication, however, was an area I found challenging. As someone who leans towards introversion and shies away from confrontation, I had to consciously work on my ability to express myself clearly, especially in my career as a businesswoman. It required effort, but improving this skill has been invaluable.

With the right values locked in, your next move should be to focus on your goals and block out the white noise. There are enough doubters and haters in the world who want you to fail already—don't join their ranks. You have to rid yourself of any limiting beliefs if you want to translate your ideas into reality.

Limiting beliefs are just that: the thoughts and beliefs you hold that prevent you from achieving all you can.

You might be thinking right now, *My parents told me I could be president when I was a kid; I can do anything if I put my mind to it.* But do you really believe that? Probably not. And sure, the presidency is unlikely, but it's not impossible. We all have limiting beliefs that we must overcome, and most of us don't even realize it. One limiting belief I used to have was thinking I was "too good for sales." I thought my skills and education would guarantee me a well-paying job beyond just earning commissions. The idea almost made me leave my first insurance interview at a captive agency when I heard it was commission-based. Thankfully, I stayed. What I've come to realize is that working on commission means you're essentially working for yourself. It opens the door to unlimited earning potential without someone else dictating your value.

Beneath this belief, however, lay a deeper fear of failure. I was apprehensive about being judged solely on my performance and worried that I might not measure up. It's a realization that many of us come to; our so-called limiting beliefs often serve as shields, protecting us from confronting our fear of failure. Recognizing this has been a pivotal step in transcending those fears and embracing the opportunities before me.

> Examples of limiting beliefs:
> - *"I'm not good at talking to people."*
> - *"No one will want what I have to sell."*
> - *"I'll never make good money."*
>
> Take those doubts and shift them to a goal-driven mindset:
> - *"I'm not good at talking to people."* → *"People are going to love to talk to me."*
> - *"No one will want what I have to sell."* → *"It may take time, but people will love my product/service."*
> - *"I'll never make good money."* → *"I am going to kill it!"*

As you become more successful, you will also find that your number of friends diminishes. All it takes is a simple Google search on the loneliness that comes with success, and you'll see 32 million results that reinforce how common social alienation is when you start to succeed. Whether it's caused by jealous feelings, limited time, or a dismissal of your personal standards being "too high," don't be surprised if your collection of friends and acquaintances lessens to a loyal few. There will always be those people who want you to do well, just not better than them. Your true friends will be the ones who stick around through the losses *and* the wins.

If you're a woman in business, you've already had your fair share of "boys' clubs." The closed doors and smug faces are another obstacle standing in your way. And, even worse, you may be conditioned to doubt yourself and your business vigor, leaving you scrambling to reach your full potential. If you've done the market research, you've thought through your ideas, then move with confidence. You've got this. Embrace the grind.

Too many people see the clock turn 5 p.m. and are ready to call it quits. Those are the same people who are later surprised when their business doesn't take off, or worse, slides into eventual failure. They blame outside forces and circumstances without looking at the big picture. Ninety-five percent of business is possessing the mental fortitude to keep pushing forward. When I first started insurance work, I was dialing (i.e., calling and speaking to leads) day in and day out. I had no client book established—that takes time to build—and was faced with rejection more often than I would have liked. Think about it this way: If I called 400 people a day, I may have talked to 15. After talking to those 15, about 5 of them would want me to send over some quotes. Out of those 5, *maybe* 1 would purchase from me. Those sound like grim odds, however, that one sale might equal $1,000 in commission. And on top of that, I did my calls around school pickups, making dinner for my kids, and helping with homework.

As for my e-commerce businesses, I had even more limited time to dedicate to them—but I didn't use that as an excuse. When my husband settled down to a movie after a long day, I spent those nights on my laptop doing research and business development. Even two years into Elysian Parfum and Execuluxe®, the "grind" never stops. You'll likely have to juggle multiple jobs and roles until your business can stand on its own. If your mindset isn't as focused and resilient as it needs to be, take the time to do the work. Your business hangs on your ability to persevere through challenges, efficiently problem solve, and inspire employees and customers alike to believe in your ideas.

Imposter Syndrome

I've had my own struggles with imposter syndrome. I wasn't raised in a household of powersuits and nepotism—I had to work hard for everything I've earned. For the longest time, I had the credentials but not the confidence. In fact, when I wrote *Soul Beneficiary* in 2021, I still didn't feel qualified to speak on insurance despite my success in the industry. While I had founded Inspired Insurance Solutions and worked my way up to run and own a hundred million dollar plus agency, I still felt like an imposter. After all, I'd been in the field for less than a decade; who was I to talk? I eventually realized that, if I wanted to grow my business, I had to overcome these feelings.

It's important to recognize when you're experiencing imposter syndrome as a product of your insecurities versus an awareness of your knowledge gaps. If you're unsure which is the cause, take a look at these questions—do they sound like questions you constantly grapple with?

- Do you agonize over even the smallest mistakes or flaws in your work?
- Do you attribute your success to luck or outside factors?
- Are you sensitive to even constructive criticism?
- Even when you are given positive feedback, do you always find something to criticize about yourself and/or your work?
- Do you fear that you cannot live up to set expectations?
- Do you feel like you will inevitably be found out as a phony?
- Do you downplay your own expertise, even in areas where you are genuinely more skilled than others?

- Do you demand more from yourself than you would from anyone else?
- Do you set expectations that you find you can never achieve?[1]

If this sounds like you, you may be struggling with imposter syndrome. Don't fret, imposter syndrome is a perfectly natural feeling, especially if you've launched a new business idea, risen to a new position of power, or taken a chance in other ways. Women in particular are burdened by these feelings of inadequacy. That said, if you don't address them, they will become a barrier to your success. The best you can do is to confront imposter syndrome head-on. Acknowledge these feelings, first to yourself and then to others. Work through your insecurities by assessing your abilities and creating a plan to supplement any knowledge you may be lacking. If you're constantly comparing yourself to others, stop that. Each person is on their own path to success, and you bring your own strengths to the table. Overcoming imposter syndrome takes time, so focus on the baby steps of confidence building.

If these feelings persist and you start to feel like everything is stacked against you and that you can't succeed at all, it may be more than imposter syndrome. It's worth talking to a professional to help you differentiate whether it's simple imposter syndrome or perhaps something more serious.

While I can now confidently walk into an insurance conference with my head high and a strong presence, I once again experienced imposter syndrome when launching my e-commerce business. My passion and focus were intact, but I once again felt underqualified. After all, I wasn't some master perfumer or a famed bag designer. It would have been easy to give up early on, but I buckled down instead. I dove all in, taking online courses, watching how-to videos on YouTube, and reading everything I could get my hands on. I traveled to California to visit a perfume academy and learned to mix my original scents firsthand. It was a transformative experience. With each passing month, I became more confident and capable as a founder of Elysian Parfum and Exculuxe®. That wouldn't have been possible if I had just given up. I had to confront my fears, acknowledge my shortcomings, and do the work to become a perfumer in my own right. Two years ago, I never would have thought this possible. Yet, here I am. And, if you can do the work to dismantle your imposter syndrome, you'll enjoy your own successes.

The Best Way to "Win" is to Overcome

Success in any field is often accompanied by naysayers and doubt. That's true for every person, regardless of the industry or experience. With the right mindset, you'll easily be able to brush aside these comments and uncertainties, but if you suffer from imposter syndrome, such things can knock you off track.

I'm no stranger to these experiences, but I've thankfully developed a thick enough skin to push through. I once had a woman say to my face, "I just had to let you know that I would *NEVER* buy that bag." Sure, she could have stayed quiet, but her comment was a good test of my mindset. Old Jessi would have gone through an intense spiral of doubt—*Are my bags too expensive? Do people need so many options?*—but my inner strength brushed aside the comment and laughed it off. Clearly, she wasn't my target audience!

Depending on who you ask, there are a million things you need to succeed: this planner, that journal, this book, that course, etc. And while these resources can help you get your business off the ground, all you ultimately need is a steadfast belief that you can achieve. The best thing you can do for your business is to develop an impenetrable mindset. The mind is a powerful tool, and it can often be your worst enemy—or you can make it your best asset. When you learn to step out of your own way and allow yourself to do the work, you might find that success will follow.

CHAPTER FOUR
FIGURE OUT YOUR FINANCES

One of my biggest fears when starting Execuluxe® and Elysian Parfum was having too little product for my audience. Consumer attention is valuable and can't be wasted. I was so concerned about meeting every single need that I overbought. Luckily for me, this mistake was marginal, but, for a less accomplished entrepreneur, the consequences can be disastrous. According to *Forbes* Councils Member Anissa Jones, the top two business "killers" are having too much overhead (buying too much) and having limited or unreliable cash flow. Finances are treacherous for new businesses, particularly if you don't have another job to fall back on.

When I first started my insurance work, that was my only source of income. I spent hours on the phone trying to sell policies and build my client book. Soon though, I went from surviving on $250 a week in unemployment benefits and food stamps to clearing six figures my first year in insurance. The hard work came first, then the financial success. This is how most entrepreneur journeys are. I know that many people are drawn to an entrepreneurial life for the freedom of time, but many don't realize that it is earned. It takes a while to be able to start relishing in that aspect of business ownership.

Fast forward to my e-commerce days—my insurance agents and agency come first, but at night, I spend most of my time designing, fine-tuning, and growing my two e-commerce ventures. I had built up residual income from my insurance business to invest in my e-commerce brands.

There are still risks I take, but the stakes aren't so high compared to others trying to make their new business their main source of income. It's a delicate balance. Invest too little and you won't attract your audience; invest too much and your bank account will be too cash-strapped to handle the costs. You have to walk a pretty fine line, so you better come equipped with the right shoes.

Very few people start out with their attention wholly focused on their new ventures. They're often working a "standard" job and building this business on the side. Regardless of whether you have a steady source of income to support you or you're trying to make a living solely on this, each cost counts. For me, a financial mistake I made with my e-commerce businesses was taking on too many products right away. I don't regret it—I wanted my customers to have enough choices to find the product best suited to them—but I did learn from it. My bags in particular had all these variations of style, color, material. I have backpacks, crossbody bags, padfolios, laptop cases, and duffel bags, plus the main roller bag.

Yes, they were selling, but the labor of designing these options, ensuring their quality, actively selling them, and packaging and sending them off—all of that wasn't necessary in the beginning. I definitely could have started off with fewer options and grown them incrementally. Of course, I didn't know then which designs and products would be big sellers. I was creating designs and trying to learn along the way. It wasn't until later, once I had already started the business, that I saw which designs sold more than others.

If you're at the product decision-making stage, take my experience into consideration. It's easy to get swept away in the excitement, especially if you're passionate about your project, but you can always introduce more products after your initial launch—that's better than becoming bogged down by all of the choices and expenses!

Overspending in the beginning can be a problem for many new businesses, but the best way to avoid this pitfall is to get a handle on your finances through budgeting and understanding the true financial breakdown of your business. That is what this chapter is all about.

Break in Your Budget

A budget is the first line of defense for keeping your finances in order. Even with my research, I didn't think my e-commerce business was going to cost as much as it did. I had a mental budget for production—I'm not a ledger or spreadsheet person—but there were many hidden costs I hadn't anticipated.

The small stuff adds up. I knew I wanted nice packaging that would reinforce my brand, so you start with your perfume. People are paying for the liquid, but you can't deliver the liquid without the bottle. And you want the bottle to look nice. Then you need a label to communicate your business name. Plus, you'll need a lid to protect the sprayer. With those pieces in place, you can't ship it with just the bottle bouncing around. You'll need to have good packaging and shipping supplies.

Another cost to consider is how the products will arrive at your home—are you going to pay someone to organize the shipping from overseas to your home? My first time around, I paid an importer to handle the goods as they came through US Customs, and he also arranged for delivery. The initial order was quite large since it contained the foundational products of my businesses, but I've since taken on that responsibility myself.

I've since learned that here are two options for delivery: EXW (Ex Works), which places the burden of time and money on the buyer, who also has to arrange for transportation, and FOB (Free on Board), where the seller is responsible for transporting the goods to a place designated by the buyer. It costs more to choose this warehouse-to-door approach than warehouse-to-port, but it does relieve the stress of shipping since it's all handled for you. If you are launching a physical product, be sure to review your budget before you make this decision.

There's also import taxes. These are quite hefty, so be sure to talk to your manufacturer if they aren't in the United States and find out your import taxes *before* buying your products. It was only when I finished ordering my 10,000 pieces of luggage/purses that the manufacturer told me about import taxes. Boy, was I surprised! So be sure to understand and incorporate that extra cost into your budget prior to placing your order.

This example is specific to e-commerce, but the point is applicable across the board: Some things you'll only find out along the way, and these lessons might cost you. This is why it's so important to learn all you can, but you're still not always going to know everything ahead of time. To plan for the unplannable expenses, you have to be aware that these things can happen and take that into account when budgeting.

Before I started, I was prepared for the production costs of the items themselves, but I sorely underestimated the follow-through expenses. That's why it's really important to pick an item that has enough of a profit margin to make up those costs. Not only is there the cost of the actual item, but there's shipping from the manufacturer, packaging, marketing, advertising, and photography. There's so much that goes into launching your own brand, and that's why I harp on the importance of ensuring it's something you're passionate about.

A good division of cost is to allocate 25 percent for marketing, save another 30 percent for taxes, and keep a balance of 20 percent for supply and inventory reordering, leaving you with a 25 percent profit—a good chunk of change for your labor. We all wish we could have 100 percent profit, but that's not how businesses work. So, if you see someone online saying they made a million a year off their brand-new business, it's safe to say it's more likely that they profited $250,000—which is still very good.

Cash-In and Cash-Flow

For some businesses, a pre- or soft launch is a great way to snag some cash flow. If you don't have expendable cash in the early stages of your business, you can use sales from a pre-launch to fund the cost of the materials. I took this avenue for my luxury bags, offering a pre-sale the summer before it officially launched in January of 2023. This shouldered some of the costs associated with producing my bags and allowed me to successfully get Execuluxe® moving. I didn't do a soft launch for the fragrances because with those I needed to utilize UGC (user-generated content) marketing, and I couldn't do that without the tangible item first.

As for sales, Execuluxe® and Elysian Parfum once again require different plans of action. Execuluxe® is built around the idea of luxury and functionality—that's my marketing approach. If I constantly discount the bags, it lowers the perceived value of them. Plus, each purchase already includes three accessories. In a rare occurrence, I do offer a bundle discount, or sometimes a special holiday discount, but it's not often. By limiting my sales, I maintain my brand of luxury without damaging my profits.

Now, the fragrances have sales much more often. Perfumes are already difficult to sell online because people want to smell before they buy, so by offering sales or the discovery sets which feature samples of many different scents, I can mitigate this challenge. I have sales for most of the major holidays: Memorial Day, Mother's Day, Father's Day, you get the idea. Take advantage of any chance you have to get in front of your audience using some sort of discount or coupon. It's crucial to lure them in to shop, particularly if you don't have a brand following already.

A major component of this is reasonably pricing your items for your chosen audience *and* the cost of production. I've always heard that if you buy something for one dollar, you should sell it for three dollars. Regardless of the specifics, it's common sense that you need to take the cost of production, add in your labor, and choose the appropriate pricing for that. Don't forget to factor in the costs of marketing and your social media campaigns! Cash flow is another reason why selecting a sustainable business idea is so crucial.

I recently considered breaking into clothing. I took my idea to the internet, researching clothing e-commerce, such as blazers, professional outfits, etc. Everything I saw was really expensive to produce just one piece—$15 was the lowest cost, and while it was nice, it wasn't *nice*. At the max, I figured I could sell it for $49. That sounds like a good $30 profit, but it fails to consider the shipping costs, import taxes, and packaging. Once I added those in, the pricing versus production cost just didn't balance out enough to justify the labor I'd put into the clothing line. Perhaps I'll revisit the idea in the future and find a way to make my clothing unique, but for now, I'm plenty busy with Elysian Parfum and Execuluxe®.

The bottom line for pricing is to know your worth. Know the cost of production, but don't forget to factor in your time as well. Many people comment that my luxury bags are too expensive. What they fail to consider, though, is that (1) if you think they're too expensive, then you are likely not who I made them for, and (2) the cost to find high-quality, functional, and stylish materials, in addition to the size of the bag, the added roller, and the accessories all contribute to this. Plus, the bags are much heavier and add increased shipping costs and import taxes.

The Weight of Taxes

Taxes are the grim reality for every individual, but it's particularly stressful for business owners. Some people go about their year without consideration for taxes and then have to fork over money when tax season hits. I'd personally rather prepare for taxes year-round by saving 30 percent of my income to lower that tax burden. It's rare that taxes are as high as 30 percent, but this goal adds some built-in cushion to tackle the unknown.

On top of this, I recommend carefully maintaining your receipts. So much can be written off as a business expense, which can reduce your overall taxes. Your phone, WiFi, maybe even a portion of your mortgage or rent (if you work from home)—these can all be written off. If you're unsure if something qualifies as a write-off, you can ask your accountant or tax person.

One crucial piece of advice for business owners is to engage a dependable tax specialist. In my initial stages, I erred by hiring an individual off the street who professed to have extensive experience. After handling my 2018 taxes, I assumed everything was in order. However, a change came when I employed a new specialist who was recommended by a trusted associate. Upon reviewing my past records, they identified a significant error in my 2018 tax filings. This oversight had led to an overpayment, and thanks to the new specialist's intervention, I was owed a substantial refund of that overpayment. This revelation underscored the impact such a mistake could have had on my business's finances over time.

This experience taught me the value of professional expertise in tax matters. The specialist I chose works with a reputable firm and has earned my complete trust. This is the level of professionalism and reliability every business owner should seek in a tax advisor. Even after relocating to Georgia, I consulted with him to ensure that my move wouldn't affect our working relationship—that's how important he's become to me, and he continues to be a pivotal figure in my financial decision-making process.

I strongly advise against attempting to manage business taxes independently to save costs. The complexity of business taxation far exceeds that of personal taxes, and the potential for error is not worth the minimal savings. Opting for professional assistance allows me to dedicate my energy to what I love most: growing my business ventures.

The Finance Defense

We touched on LLCs in the investment chapter, but I wanted to explore them a little more here. Before I launched Elysian Parfum and Execuluxe®, I created an LLC called Luxe Group Designs. This protects me from liability and creates a division between my personal finances and the income from my businesses. That separate bank account is a mandatory step for establishing your business's finances. For this reason, it's important that you choose the right bank for your needs.

I first considered Bank United. They have a good reputation and are fairly accessible. I really liked their personable approach and felt they took our client-representative relationship seriously. Unfortunately, I felt their technology was severely lacking and didn't meet my needs. I'm no tech wizard, but the world of business does require a certain level of technological skill no matter what. I instead chose Chase Bank to handle this major undertaking. Their technology is incredible, and they can meet my needs. The trade-off, in my opinion, is that if you call in or go to the bank, you're treated like a regular person, not a years-long client. There are pros and cons to each bank, so be sure to understand your own needs and decide what's the highest priority for you. There are thousands of banks out there, so search for the right one.

A last consideration for your finances is a backup fund. It's the emergency, what-if-the-car-breaks-down fund, but it's for your business. This is far more crucial if you plan to make your business your primary source of income. For me, I work in insurance and have no plans to stop that career any time soon. E-commerce is a passion that I've added to my day rather than being a replacement for my work. Not everyone is this set-up though, and they often have to decide between one or the other. That's a big risk, and you have to take steps to protect yourself.

Most advisors recommend a minimum of three month's worth of operation costs saved away in some type of backup fund. This account should remain untouched unless absolutely necessary. Three months of operations is obviously a huge amount of money to save. Start small but remain consistent with your savings—you can consider that payment almost like a paycheck to your business every two weeks. Eventually, you can reach that three to six month level of savings, but for now, take the steps you can to build your savings.

Commit to the Finances

When you're starting to market your business, there's a lot of upfront expenditure. It's unlikely anyone knows who you are at this point, so you have to capture their attention (and hold it) *and* earn their trust. That's not a small demand considering the competitive market. You have to run brand awareness campaigns to grow your email and text list and showcase your products and/or services. Marketing has a lot to do with building and adding value to your products so people can really see how luxurious they are. Eventually, you'll reach a point where the brand and products speak for themselves. I've not reached that point yet, but I am on my way. Once you achieve this, you can dial back your marketing and focus on organic growth, diverting that excess cash flow elsewhere.

As you consider the nuances of finances, make sure you choose a direction that allows you to scale *and* has a large profit margin. You never want to reach a point where your product price just barely covers the cost of production and doesn't finance your labor input. If your business isn't profitable, you have to keep making changes until it is. On a different note, I can assure you that paying taxes is always going to make you feel sick to your stomach—that feeling isn't one of failure, just the reality of business. You can mitigate that feeling a little by saving 30 percent throughout the year in preparation for tax season, but the best antidote is to hire a professional you can trust to have your best interests at heart. Keep in mind that you can write off a multitude of things for your business that will lessen your tax burden.

At the end of the day, the finances are the stressful but necessary parts of entrepreneurship. That's why I always say you have to be passionate about your business. Otherwise, you'll run for the hills when you either see minimal profit or go negative. It's the intrinsic reward that will motivate you to square your shoulders, lift your head, and work harder the next day.

CHAPTER FIVE

THE BASICS OF YOUR BRAND

You work hard; you deserve this. You don't need to shoulder everything. The minute you shed your handful of bags—a purse with your wallet, a messenger bag holding your laptop and notes, a lunchbox packed for a long day on the go—in favor of an Execuluxe® Rollerbrief, you experience this brand. Gone are your days of juggling bags and feeling overwhelmed by responsibilities; the Execuluxe® brand promotes a functional reward for all of your sacrifice.

    I refer to my bag and fragrance brands as affordable luxury, which is based on my own shopping experiences. I won't shy away from saying that I like nice things, but I've never been a label chaser. I like to occasionally splurge on a designer pair of shoes just as much as I enjoy finding something at TJMaxx. It's not about the brand for me; I simply want good quality products that won't wipe out my bank account. And when I launched my e-commerce endeavors, I wanted to give the same accessibility to my customers.

    As you embark on your brand, embrace the basics. Keep your brand clean, simple, and, of course, authentic to the core values of your business. When you make decisions, consider how all the business elements support your brand as you build it up. For me, every Execuluxe® decision I make has an established, professional woman on-the-go in mind. Elysian Parfum is similar, focusing on people who prioritize their self-care and want to step into their days smelling good and don't mind spending a little more on a niche brand. Finally, Inspired Insurance Solutions, LLC, adds humanity to the industry by placing clients in control of their plans. It's always my priority to let them know that they are in control of their own insurance plan, and I tailor every policy to ensure each and every client's needs are met. The brands are straightforward, and I keep their tenets at the center of every decision I make for each business.

The Steps

Some entrepreneurs prepare to launch their businesses and already know what their brand will entail. While I had the core ideas in mind, I still considered all sorts of brands: How would I communicate the brand? What's the underlying message? This reflection is all part of the process. Defining your brand is more than a simple decision; there are many elements to consider.

You first start with your idea. Consider:
- How can you distill your values into a distinct brand?
  - Can a prospective customer/client understand your company and its ethos from your website? An ad? Just the slogan? Great brands of the world like Disney and Nike, for example, have such a masterful hold on their respective entities that even an alien can understand Disney's magic-making mission and Nike's endeavor to empower the everyman just by their logos alone.

- Is this proposed brand idea authentic for your products?
    - As an example, a company that boasts of its environmental work should hardly use plastic and other wasteful materials that contradict their environmental promise. Your products have to "walk the walk" that your brand espouses; otherwise, you have a major incongruency that will confuse and turn away customers.
- Does this brand image align with your passions and values?
    - Customers and employees alike will know if you're simply going through the motions and are not committed to your brand's vision.

After you have this initial foundation, you should shift your attention to the internet. Hit Google search, go to Pinterest, explore Instagram—what images resonate with you and embody your brand? Collect these images and start to mentally build out your vision. How do you want the brand to come across? From this research, you can select the colors and hues to complement your brand. Compile everything into a mood board and brand guide.

You want to make the brand come alive before you take it to the public. This means integrating your brand into the business: coordinating photoshoots (where applicable), using the brand colors throughout your website, and creating a logo that appropriately conveys your brand.

Put It into Practice

Every business decision you make should be made through the lens of your brand. Even if it's not the most original product to sell, I chose to offer discovery scent sets so that customers can sample their preferences before buying a larger bottle. Elysian is currently an online-only store, and as such, I have to acknowledge that people don't often purchase fragrances without knowing the scent profiles and how they wear. Since I offer affordable luxury, it's practical to compensate for the online factor by providing a chance to play around with different scents to find the best fit.

Take packaging as another example. Think about the last time you felt the thrill of a package hitting your door. Was the rush of delivery followed by a plain plastic-bagged item inside the bland cardboard box, or did you open your order to find the items wrapped like your very own personal present? Even the most everyday purchases have a certain extra "sparkle" when they arrive in custom packaging. You can tell when your order from Amazon, Thriftbooks, etc. has arrived before you even open the box. The effect of branded packaging is underrated but powerful nevertheless.

I want every client to have a transformative unboxing experience. To make this happen, I have customized shipping boxes and printed tissue paper. Each purse and every fragrance bottle from the Lineage Collection gets its own satin bag, customized box, and lid as well. All of these pieces together create an auspicious experience that truly conveys the luxury feel of my brands.

As for my insurance business, you can see our brand embedded in the way we engage with our agents. It's one thing to be exemplary for clients; it's next level to apply this same brand of care to your employees. A couple of years ago, I actually went and got a life coaching certificate, and I started incorporating what I learned there into my Friday trainings with my team. "Coffee and Crew" is our weekly forum. For the first 20 minutes, I incorporate broader life coaching topics, like setting goals, using vision boards, how to talk to yourself, prepping for situations, establishing a strong mindset—you get the point. Then, the last 40 minutes are dedicated entirely to the agents. They can share their concerns, issues, ideas—whatever it may be, we talk it through together. Some people would call this basic management, but if you were to cross over the threshold of most insurance offices, the cutthroat environment would leave you uneasy. Just as the Inspired Insurance Solutions brand is built on transparent camaraderie with our clients, I require that same philosophy to apply to my team.

Logo

A logo is, in a sense, the face of the brand. Without the physical introduction to your brand at a brick and mortar store, you have to create a virtual brand environment in just a few moves. The logo needs to become an emblem of trust and a representation of your brand's promise.

A logo is the constant that accompanies social media posts, purchases, packaging, advertisements, and more. As such, a well-crafted logo is an indispensable tool in your arsenal. I do have a flair for fashion, but I was out of my depth trying to create a polished logo, so I used the affordable resource, 99 Designs. I entered a description of my businesses, prescribed the tone I was looking for, and watched the ideas pour in. Once I selected my favorite design, it took eight iterations to reach the version I use today.

They say a picture is worth a thousand words, and a logo needs to communicate the right message about your brand. Unlike a 500-word company description, a logo should inspire a connection between consumers and the business while communicating the values and brand personality. As you brainstorm your logo design, keep it:

1. Simple
2. Relevant
3. Memorable
4. Timeless
5. Versatile

Be mindful as you select your palette colors—certain colors evoke reactions. Red, for instance, is seen as an intense signal of passion, energy, and potentially danger. Blue is considered very peaceful and sympathetic but sometimes passive. The list goes on and on, creating a whole psychology of color, and this alters the impact of logos for sales: Colors are proven to increase brand recognition by up to 80 percent, with 92 percent of consumers saying that visual factors are the most important marketing component.[2, 3] Don't leave the logo's impact up to chance—do your research to see what messages you're conveying and what emotions you're invoking. The payoff will be worthwhile. If you're the creative type, you can design your own logo (a resource list is included at the end of this chapter), but if you're like me, a logo is best left to the professionals. After all, it'll become the first touchpoint with your audience.

Managing an Online Presence

As a business, you have to make a strong virtual impression, particularly through social media. According to Statista, global social commerce sales reached nearly one billion dollars in 2022 and $1.298 billion in 2023. That, combined with the average person spending two plus hours on social media per day, can be a driving force in your sales.

Here's the chance to become more than a faceless corporate brand—your personable presence is what can differentiate you from your competitors. I try to remain transparent with my audience; they don't know the nuts and bolts of the costs, suppliers, and packaging, but I provide a snapshot into my life and the process. I show the human side, just as I speak to clients as humans rather than cash cows. I'm honest with who I am. I'm a working mom, and I don't hide that. My bags in particular were made to solve my problems: an overabundance of stuff I was trying to juggle on business trips. As a longtime fan of fashion, I didn't want to sacrifice sleek for functional. Instead, I created bags that are sexy but serve their purpose. For my fragrances, I clearly state that Jenni, my sister, is the inspiration for the products. The brand is authentic to my mission and to who I am; that's why my business is memorable.

Social media is a crucial part of the online equation, one that we'll explore further in chapter seven. As for the brand part, I write out those elements in my messaging. Be sure your message isn't falling on deaf ears though—you need to lock in your ideal customer.

Ideal Customer

If you close your eyes, can you envision your ideal customer? What are their wants, needs, and fears? In what online space do they congregate? These are basic questions that are at the crux of your ideal customer. Whether you have a specific person in mind or need to create a fictional depiction, analyzing and understanding your ideal customer is the path forward to successful sales.

With Execuluxe®, I imagine customers similar to me. They likely commute to their job, have a large workload they carry daily, or are on the road frequently for business trips, hence the need for a trolley bag. In addition, they're stylish people who care about their appearance, dressing to impress. A simple and bulky black roller bag would diminish this polished look, while my luxury bags elevate their personal brand. With this in mind, I know that my bags are not accessible for everyone. While inexpensive for the quality of the bag and stylish design, the price point is likely out of the average price range for most people. Instead, my ideal customer is someone who is doing well in their career and has the necessary expendable income to make such a purchase. Time and again, I'm asked about the cost of the bags—or left online comments from customers who want them but can't afford them. My response? You're likely not the intended audience, and that's okay. I love TJ Maxx and Target as much as the next person, but when I want to travel in style on business trips, I take my roller bag.

Sydney Wilson

Who is she? Sydney is a single mom of two in a high-powered career. Between her accounting job and the kids' extracurriculars, her schedule is always booked up.

What does she want? She wants order in the chaos. Whether it's having a notepad on hand during meetings or whipping out an after-school snack for her kids, Sydney wants to feel prepared for every situation.

What does she need? Sydney needs pockets for her pen, pocketbook, snacks, a place to slide her phone into, and a section for her laptop and paperwork. It all needs to look tidy and, above all, chic.

> *What does she fear?* One of the worst things Sydney can imagine is being unprepared. She doesn't want to be the messy single mom that so many employers expect and dismiss. Sydney has worked hard for her career and wants to prove it, even when she has to slide into "mom mode" after work.
>
> *Takeaway:* With Sydney in mind, I can picture the bags' design more easily. We're looking for accessibility with a polished look. Plus, the accessories can reduce stress and clutter for "Sydney," whether she chooses the lunch tote, the laptop case, or any of my other options. Your ideal customer should become a symbol of those you're looking to serve. Let their wants, needs, and fears become the compass of your decision-making.

Meanwhile, at Elysian Parfum we have evolved our identity as a more boutique experience that offers hand-crafted scents in small batches that are completely unique, elevating our brand to be a luxury in and of itself. Every perfume in our collection is no less than an olfactory masterpiece designed for those seeking a brand-new, complex, and luxurious scent. With this in mind, our ideal customer is someone who fully appreciates fragrances and everything that goes into creating them. While our price point is not quite as high as some other niche fragrances, this customer isn't looking for "accessible luxury"; they're looking for something new entirely. That is what Elysian Parfum offers.

Dani Thompson

Who is she? Dani Thompson is a discerning individual with a refined taste for the unique and luxurious aspects of life. She seeks authenticity and quality in her choices, from her wardrobe to her fragrance collection.

What does she want? Dani desires exclusivity, craving scents that not only complement her personality but also set her apart in any gathering.

What does she need? She needs a fragrance that resonates with her individuality and enhances her presence—a scent that is as distinct and memorable as her persona.

What does she fear? Dani fears the commonplace and the generic; she is wary of blending into the background or coming across as one-dimensional. Her fear is rooted in the loss of her unique identity amidst the sea of mass-produced fragrances. She is looking for a scent that upholds her distinctiveness, ensuring she remains unforgettable.

Takeaway: Elysian Parfum provides the perfect solution to Dani's desires and needs. With its focus on hand-crafted, small-batch perfumes, Elysian Parfum offers her the exclusivity and unique identity she seeks in a fragrance. It promises to elevate her personal scent profile, ensuring she stands out with sophistication and elegance. Dani Thompson is the ideal client for Elysian Parfum, as she embodies the essence of the brand's target market: individuals who value luxury, uniqueness, and personal expression through their choice of fragrance.

With my insurance company, my main audience these days is primarily agents. I recruit quality humans, train them to my standards, and then they carry the brand onward in their work. These agents speak to clients the way I always did when I first started as an insurance agent. The target audience here is pretty much anyone, with the exception of those on welfare, people who receive Medicaid, veterans who receive VA benefits, etc., as they are already covered by governmental programs. Instead, the focus is on people who work and have an income but may have some financial limitations that require crafty maneuvering to create a sustainable insurance plan for them. I always push the importance of an open conversation, asking about their fears, needs, and concerns. I interject personal stories and avoid sterile, scripted discussions. Every contact is meant to be a pleasurable experience. Regardless of your field, you have to keep your ideal customer vision in mind as you proceed.

Elle Williams

Who is she? Elle is a 54-year-old woman who's just changed careers. After decades as a teacher, she's living out her dream of being a tour guide at a historical site.

What does she want? She's looking for coverage of basic medications, along with good price points on office visits.

What does she need? Elle needs this to be a headache-free, easy process so she can focus on the things in life that bring her joy. Especially as she is getting older, she needs to know that she can access healthcare now and that she will be covered in the worst-case scenarios.

> *What does she fear?* She fears a plan that is so expensive it sucks away her savings before she even hits retirement. At the same time, she also fears not having the safety net of a good insurance policy to protect her now and in the future.
>
> *Takeaway:* Elle is a client story I've heard many times. People are busy with their lives and shouldn't have to worry about their insurance. After speaking with Elle, I'll know that a thorough, no-frills plan is what will suit her best. The tour guide position is great, but it does mean she'll be on her feet a lot, walking across irregular terrain. Like many people, she'll need yearly check-ins, as well as medications and coverage for potential emergencies. As I craft "Elle's" options, I'll keep her informed of the prices and coverage, creating "Good, Better, Best" plans for her to choose from.

If you want to make it in the business world, you need to understand your ideal customer. Price too high and you'll lose them; price too low and your ideal customer will overlook you entirely. Speak to their needs, and you'll earn that customer loyalty. And that can be priceless.

Conclusion

A brand acts as the compass and manifesto for your business—it presents your values and story to the market, and, if done correctly, it can become a familiar and trusted symbol for your audience. I always say that communication is an irreplaceable pillar for a business; after all, how can a customer trust you and make purchases if they have to jump through hoops to talk to a real person (and not a bot)? "Treat people the way you want to be treated." It may sound cliché, but people have an exceptional BS meter. If your brand is inauthentic, and you don't conduct business with the values you spout, you won't be able to fake it with customers. Carry the respect of your brand to your messaging and business interactions. By staying true to your brand, your business will come alive.

CHAPTER SIX
MAKE THE MOST OF YOUR MARKETING

I've always had a fascination with marketing, even from an early age. At around 11 years old, I received a booklet in the mail from the Sunshine Sales Club. It was one of those campaigns where you could earn points to buy things from their catalog if you successfully sold items from their magazine. I sold stationary, candy, knickknacks, and other items to people all around where I lived. Getting the sale made my little heart soar. I used those points to get a boombox, a clear phone, and then a heart-shaped phone, which was all the rage back in the '90s. Eventually, I had gotten myself everything I could ever want from their catalog and started making two dollars per item. You could say I was super motivated to make those sales.

I enlisted my little sister and our cousin in the endeavor. They were a little shy to knock on doors, but I had no such qualms. I even came up with a catchy jingle that we sang any time someone opened the door. It's not an exaggeration to say that we rode our bikes to hundreds of houses across the neighborhood. It was my first introduction to marketing, and it may very well have been the reason I went into marketing later on.

That initial spark from my door-to-door marketing efforts turned into a full-fledged passion once I started my own e-commerce business selling homemade candles in 2001. It became clear that my interest was in the marketing side: I loved naming the candles and deciding on the labels—I even established a fabulous website despite the limitations of the internet at the time. I taught myself enough HTML code to be able to customize my website and link it up to Mal's e-commerce (which was our Shopify back in the day). Social media was in its infancy, smart phones didn't even exist, and the online world in general was less accessible. After six years, I put e-commerce on the back burner and focused on the corporate grind.

My marketing education didn't end there. Before I entered the insurance world, I actually worked in marketing for a salon studio concept company. I helped design flyers and handled their social media. The company was a salon studio that acted as an umbrella company for individual hair stylists, nail techs, and other beauty service providers who paid rent to use the space. Many of them were excellent at what they did and very creative, but some lacked the business acumen to get enough clients to make a living, which led to a higher turnover rate. So I proposed that we start a school that essentially taught these salon professionals how to market for themselves, build their websites, interact on social media, and build clientele. That endeavor, which consisted of six courses the salon professionals could take, did more than empower these small business owners; it improved salon retention, thereby stabilizing the cash flow as well.

I learned a lot in my role as director of marketing, so unlike many other e-commerce professionals and entrepreneurs, I have a slight edge when it comes to marketing and PR work for businesses. But my experience is your advantage too—I'm not here to gatekeep my knowledge.

Understanding the Basics

A common mistake people make is lumping in branding with marketing. Think of them as a Venn diagram—there's some overlap, but they are distinct facets. As you saw in the previous chapter, branding is the essence of your business; it's how you determine the XYZ of your mission, products, and company. Marketing is the follow-through, your implementation and execution. At its core, marketing is about understanding and addressing the needs, fears, and desires of your audience. Consider it your chance to tell a story, using compelling narratives to illustrate your brand's uniqueness and demonstrate why your brand matters in the lives of your customers.

If you plan to take the DIY approach, marketing may seem like an overwhelming endeavor. But with the evolution of the internet comes an increase in available tools, which will alleviate the stress considerably. That said, not every marketing tool out there is worth the investment. Start off with a reasonable budget to incorporate the basics, perhaps running ads on spaces like Facebook, Instagram, Google. There are very few ways for new e-commerce businesses to gain traffic, so you have to try and increase the number of touchpoints through ads.

One of the best platforms I've found is Shopify. It has everything you need to build your online store, outline your brand, and manage your customer base. Shopify is like having a handy assistant in my corner: It creates a log for each IP that visits your product. This includes how many times consumers visit before buying, how long it takes to "convert" them before they buy your product, if they're repeat buyers, etc. This data can be priceless, particularly to a well-versed entrepreneur. On top of this data, Shopify creates profiles and email lists, allowing you to easily connect with your audience. In conjunction with an email campaign, you should also engage with SMS. I send out a message one to two times a week to maintain the buyer-seller relationship. Be careful not to be too frequent though, as that can have an adverse effect on customers and annoy them into unsubscribing. I do not recommend messaging more than two per week, and only doing that occasionally.

I also recommend ensuring you use metafields to populate the message with each person's name for an added layer of personalization. Compared to emails, text messages have an almost 100 percent open rate. Now, that doesn't directly convert to sales, but the increased exposure naturally increases product awareness, which increases the likelihood of more sales.

In today's digital age, agility and adaptability are key marketing components. Consumer behaviors and technology evolve rapidly, but you can stay with the curve by creating strategies that are customer-centric, data-driven, and flexible, allowing your brand to navigate changes and remain relevant in a competitive landscape.

Every bit of profit and some of your initial financing needs to be invested into your marketing efforts. As an unknown business, you need to catch people's attention, invite them in, and build a relationship. That requires steady and consistent effort.

As you explore the tools at your disposal, it's crucial to remember that effective marketing is not just about promoting products or services—it's about creating meaningful connections and delivering value that resonates with your target audience. This involves a deep understanding of who your customers are (your ideal customers and what the data says), what they value, and how they want to engage with your brand. I keep my demographic at the front of every decision I make. With Execuluxe®, I'm geared towards executive men and women who have to commute or travel often. They have the money to spend on a bag that will reduce their hassle without taking away from their polished appearance. Some businesses overcompensate and make their niche *too specific*. You have to leave room for adaptability in both the demographic and the product.

For Elysian Parfum, I'm geared towards the fragrance connoisseur (which is most people) who wants to smell good and isn't afraid to try new things.

The Advanced Elevator Pitch

By now, you've no doubt memorized your 60-second elevator pitch. The next step is to pull together a media kit. This builds on the elevator pitch introduction and offers a more thorough explanation of your brand and business in one convenient folder. Even though my e-commerce businesses are just a few years old, I've developed a media kit to highlight their distinctive success and corner of the market. My media kits follow this basic form:

- **Cover letter or introduction**
  - Operate under the assumption that whoever is reading this media kit knows nothing of your business. Introduce yourself and your business, and include a brief description of what your media kit aims to present. This is one of the rare places

where you can include your personality, setting the tone for the following documents.

- **Overview of the company**
  - Invite the reader into your company by reviewing its history, mission, and value statements. This is your chance to distinguish what sets your company apart from its competitors, so be sure to highlight your unique selling proposition.
- **Product and/or service descriptions**
  - Provide a brief overview of your product or service. If you have these descriptions on your website, feel free to copy those as a foundation, adding to them the features, benefits, and selling points. I recommend including images or diagrams to reinforce your brand, but be sure they are high-quality and digestible.
- **Fact sheets**
  - Consider this a bullet point profile where you can summarize the key points of your company, products, and/or services. Make these easy to read, to the point, and visually appealing.
- **Team biography**
  - Humanize your business. Who are its founders, executives, and other key team members? Delve into their experience and roles within the company. If you have professional photos, be sure to add these as well.
- **Case studies or testimonials**
  - While these can be found with a quick Google search, case studies and testimonials demonstrate the value and impact of your business.

- **Press releases**
    - Recent press releases can show the growth and prowess of your company and products.
- **Media coverage**
    - If your business has been featured in any articles, interviews, podcasts, or reviews, be sure to include that information here. A link or sample from a trusted source can enhance your credibility.
- **Any awards and recognition you may have been nominated for or received**
    - This is the chance to share any achievements that will further your business's brand.
- **High-quality images and videos**
    - Gather high-quality images of your product, services, team, or events. If applicable, include any videos of product demonstrations, interviews with team members, or promotional clips as well.
- **Contact information**
    - Make it easy for a reader to contact the business, whether it be for media inquiries, sales, or customer service. Outline any relevant names, phone numbers, and email addresses.

This may seem like a lot to pull together, but the value of a polished media kit is unmistakable. It's like a personal resume for your brand—one that you can pass around.

The Personal or Professional Approach

As you grow—or if you start with sufficient funding—you may decide to hire an ad agency instead of taking the DIY approach to marketing. While most of these tactics are easy to learn, they do require time. An agency reduces that stress, and you'll likely see an ROI sooner under their guidance. As with any business, you have to do your due diligence. Ensure the marketing agency is transparent with their work and that you get reasonable results. The simple truth is that you get what you pay for.

When you see companies that claim fantastical results for an extremely competitive price, it might just be too good to be true. Even if they claim to be based in the US, there exist many agencies who take contracts and outsource the actual work to people overseas, usually from tech-savvy India or Pakistan. Too many people have too many horror stories about agencies who promise the world, only to drastically underdeliver or even disappear once your check clears. These bad-faith businesses affect your ability to launch, waste your precious budget, and can impact your success. This is not a situation you want to find yourself in.

But it's not just a matter of rotten luck—most marketing agency nightmares can be entirely avoided by taking an active role in choosing your agency and properly researching them before signing any contracts. Don't choose the first agency you find and blindly sign on the dotted line. You should know exactly what you are getting yourself into. Read the contract and understand their deliverables, communication, and other stated expectations in the fine print. Check to see if there are any clauses that bind you to the company for any required length of time; ideally, you should always have a quick exit available in case things go south. Ask for references, and seek out as many reviews as possible from their current and former clients. It is on you to gather information and decide accordingly.

Preferably, you want to find an agency who sets realistic expectations and offers proof of results for past clients. Agencies who advise that it takes time to introduce a brand and see sales (which is absolutely true) are more likely to achieve actual success for your business than a suspiciously-cheap agency who promises you the world ever will. The road to building brand awareness is long, and you need to make sure you're teaming up with an agency who's in it for that long haul.

Something to consider when working with an agency is that you may not have to work with them forever, and you can decide to end the working relationship if they are not meeting your expectations. Sometimes you might decide that you only need an agency to help you get set up and introduce your brand, and in the course of that learn to manage the rest of the ongoing marketing tasks yourself. Sometimes you may need to "upgrade" to another agency in order to reach a new milestone or pivot your brand. Don't feel like you have to commit to your current agency for any reason other than a contract; after all, they are ultimately a "tool" within your arsenal that will drag you down if it no longer serves you.

If you are looking to do it yourself for any length of time, know that it is possible—but it will take much more time, and sometimes even more money, to learn to set up and manage your own marketing. Mistakes are inevitable and come at a price, but you will gain a lesson learned. It's all a part of the learning journey, especially when you want to gain mastery of such a massive and essential part of business.

You'll find plenty of free or low-cost resources to learn everything you need, which is fortunate because you will need to learn a *lot*. There are many different facets of marketing that you must learn, undertake, and manage when you DIY, and you also have to learn and deploy different strategies depending on where your business is at and where you want it to go. It can occupy a lot of headspace, especially when you are trying to manage all other facets of your business, but it can get easier over time. It all comes down to your priorities, values, goals, and where your time versus money is best spent. If your personal availability is greater than your cash budget and you see value in learning all of this on your own, then perhaps the DIY approach is best.

Whether you do it yourself or hire an agency, the most important factor is patience. Marketing takes time, especially when introducing a new brand and building awareness. Big-name brands like Gucci or Target didn't immediately pop into the public consciousness. It happened over time, not overnight, and it's through the same gradual process that you will bring your brand to awareness.

The biggest quantitative marker to gauge the success of your marketing is your "Return on Ad Spend," more commonly known by the acronym ROAS. The ROAS refers to how much in sales you see compared to how much you spend on ads/marketing. There are no hard and fast rules on how high your ROAS ought to be, but you should aim to see your ROAS hit or surpass the 4x level within six months of working with an agency. If you're spending $10k on ads each month, you should be seeing $40k of sales in return. This tells you if your current campaign/agency is running effectively.

However, it shouldn't be considered an empirical failure if your ROAS falls short of 4x. Rather than treating it as a sign that your efforts are not working, you can instead see it as an indication that some aspect of your marketing could benefit from some tweaking. Look for the opportunity to enhance your marketing, and you will inevitably find it.

Make the Most of Your Marketing

You don't need a degree to run effective marketing campaigns. Most tools are a few clicks away, and if technology isn't your strong suit, there's an endless supply of how-to articles, blogs, and videos. If you prefer to pass over this DIY approach, there are countless marketing companies willing to take on the brunt of the work, as I mentioned earlier. I've taken both routes, and I can't say that either one is superior. I loved the DIY approach—it put me in control, encouraged me to keep up with the trends, and helped me add my personal touch to my business. I also loved learning all the new things regarding e-commerce. Now that I'm busier, it's necessary to free up some time by diverting work to a marketing agency. It's a coin flip, but only you can decide the best path to take. Regardless, be sure to embrace the true game-changer for e-commerce: social media.

CHAPTER SEVEN

YOUR #1 TOOL: SOCIAL MEDIA

Though a relatively recent invention in the history of mankind, social media has quickly come to be a nearly universal aspect of all our daily lives. Like it or not, the fact is that social media is the inevitable starting point for all businesses in this day and age. When done right, social media is a tool you can wield to reach customers far beyond your physical reach and launch your business. Word-of-mouth promotion can only go so far; in the new digital space, there are no limits to how far you can get your business out there.

I have to credit at least some of Elysian Parfum's initial success to Instagram's perfume community. In the beginning, I created a line of dupes that replicated the popular scents from Tom Ford, Chanel, Yves Saint Laurent, and other iconic brands. These were well-received, and the community was extremely supportive of our fledgling business, but I was surprised to see that our house originals outperformed all of our well-known dupes. We pivoted to focus solely on our own originals and, when faced with higher MOQs (minimum order quantities) and higher overall costs to restock from our manufacturers, I decided to make the jump into making the perfume myself. I underwent an education with the best in the business to learn all things olfactory, and I came out confident in my decision to do it on my own. Now the originals are truly an in-house collection, and with thousands of orders in our first year, Elysian's growth shows no signs of slowing down. With so much ahead, I still look back and appreciate that Instagram and the people on there really helped build us up when we were only beginning.

Social media can make or break just about any business, especially e-commerce ones like mine. With brick-and-mortar stores on the decline and virtual sales platforms like Amazon continuing to skyrocket in popularity, the facts are clear: If you want to sell, you need to get online.

Take It Online

You might be thinking, *Well I'm not in e-commerce, so why would social media be relevant for me?* And the truth is, it's relevant for everyone. If you run a landscaping company, for example, you might be able to canvas a neighborhood with door-to-door flyers and build business that way, but you're certainly not capturing the rest of your town. You know who will, though? The competitor who has built up their social media and digital presence enough that when people search "landscaping near me," their business is the first result. Referrals from other clients might be helpful as a hairdresser, but what's even better is before-and-after hair transformations showing up on your demographic's social media feed. A restaurant that knows how to advertise its weekly specials on Instagram and interact with regulars are going to get more people in the door than a restaurant you have to call to get their hours from. Unless your target demographic falls under the one percent of people who don't own phones, every potential customer you may have is currently online, and if you want to reach them, that's where you'll have to go too.

Fortunately, social media is by nature extremely accessible, and it takes only a little bit of time, thought, and effort to set yourself up and start building your own social media presence. First, you need to decide what platforms to prioritize. While I would always recommend creating an account on any and all social media platforms to claim your business's username, you can't reasonably expect to consistently post on and actively put effort into every single platform out there. Big brands have an entire team to manage all their social media, but you are only one person and thus it's important to "work smart, not hard." Not all platforms are equal, and depending on your target demographic, some platforms will be more worth the effort than others.

Think about the typical age range, gender, socioeconomic status, geographical location, and other key features of your target demographic, and compare that to the known user stats of the most popular social media platforms. You will most likely need to do a bit of research to find and compare those numbers, but that information is readily available online. Think also about your business and what applicable "niche" it might fall into online. If you are a fantasy author whose readers are primarily Millennials and Gen Z, you should absolutely focus your efforts on TikTok and Instagram. Be sure to look up relevant hashtags for your niche. For example, #booktok is massively popular on TikTok for books, but if you're selling a media literacy course for seniors, you're probably better off investing more into Facebook. Know that you also don't have to *only* post on this one platform—once you have gained enough of an audience on one, you can more easily launch another as some of your current followers will roll into the next platform.

Once you've decided where you'll most often post, you now need to decide *what* to post. This is where some people can fall into a creative rut or find themselves camera-shy. Finding inspiration is as simple as searching the hashtags of your target demographic and seeing what other people are doing. Social media is made for trends, and you might find yourself on the viral bandwagon by posting a brand-appropriate version of that week's Harlem Shake, Renegade, or Ice Bucket Challenge. Trends, of course, are ultimately short-lived, and it's important to also balance your feed with original content. The content that tends to do best follows three key pillars: educational, inspirational, and entertaining.

Think about why influencers like PewDiePie, Charli D'Amelio, and Brittany Broski became so popular in their particular genres. There are millions of people who can game, dance, or provide commentary. What makes these three individuals stand out amongst a sea of equally talented people is their ability to connect with their audience. Their audience doesn't follow them just for what they're doing; they're following them for *them*. Humans are social creatures, and we all respond to content that allows us to see and know the person behind it. If you can connect with your audience on a personal level, you've captured their attention (and potentially their dollars) more than any other approach will.

An easy way to do this is to simply show the person behind the brand. If you can share a little bit about yourself and the backstory of your business, people are much more likely to form connections and subsequent brand loyalty. People can buy organic goat's milk soap just about anywhere, but if they see the backyard goats and the cardigan-clad retiree tending to them, they are infinitely more likely to buy from them—and buy from them exclusively. Sometimes it's the individuality and personality of a brand that brings them above competitors, so any little bit of yourself that you can show your viewers can make a big impact.

Sometimes it's as easy as turning the camera around on yourself and showing your face, which is easier said than done. For many people (especially for us women who have dealt with a lifetime of comments and criticisms about our appearances), showing themselves on camera can stir up all kinds of insecurities, which the online trolls and haters can undeniably be very cruel about. Bullies get a lot more bold when they can hide behind a keyboard and the threat of mean comments alone can make some people balk from ever even trying to post online at all.

But we should never let other people box us in and hold us back from our full potential. If you are worried about negative feedback, you can always choose to moderate or restrict your comment section. More importantly, you can even take this as an opportunity to learn to not take the meanness of other people to heart. I have heard all kinds of nasty rumors about myself in the insurance world and receive negative comments about the price or material of my Execuluxe® bags all the time, and I just let it roll off my back. As for the people who complain that Execuluxe® is too expensive, all I can say is that it's just not made for them and that they aren't the intended audience. There are plenty of people out there who have a need for this bag and value it enough to pay for it, so why should I stop and listen to people who will never buy from my brand anyway? I've grown a pretty thick skin over the years, and stuff like this doesn't even bother me anymore. Just be prepared to occasionally have to delete comments from an online troll known only as user83262938429 who has no profile pictures.

If you are camera-shy, know that filters exist, and there is absolutely no shame in using them. Especially for us women who are expected to have their hair and makeup on point 24/7, sometimes not being picture-perfect can keep us from making quality content that will help grow our platforms. Many people have suddenly been struck with inspiration for a good video, only to stop because they hadn't done their makeup that day or their hair wasn't quite right. Filters can help you achieve that polished look at any time and though some big influencers try to claim otherwise, *everyone* uses them to some extent. A little skin-smoothing or eyelash effect can go a long way to make you feel presentable and more comfortable in front of the camera, which in turn helps you focus more on the content than on how you look delivering it. Always remember that authenticity goes a long way, so don't let any of the above be a personal pain point. Most people don't care and won't judge you at all. Just be yourself, but until you get comfortable, use filters.

Of course, I would be remiss if I didn't differentiate between using a filter to be camera-ready and digitally altering your appearance to the point of unrecognition. I don't advocate for anyone to completely morph themselves like that. After all, what's the point of being on camera at all if you are presenting a completely different person? Many viewers would see that as a sort of deception and feel disconnected from the person on screen, which is totally contrary to our intent to be on camera anyways. The bottom line is that you should still look like you and to use filters at your own discretion.

The other algorithm-friendly form of content is that which encourages participation and engagement from your audience. When YouTubers sign off with "Thanks for watching and please subscribe to my channel for more videos like this one" or TikTokers throw in "Let's see if we can get this one to 40k likes," they're really inviting their viewers to engage with their content beyond just watching it. Likes, comments, shares, saves, and all other additional ways viewers can interact with the content are extremely important signals for social media algorithms to "see" that people like your content, which can prompt the algorithm to then start showing your content to more users and feature your content in relevant hashtags.

If you find the shameless plugs of "Smash that like button" or "Don't forget to hit follow" to be a little too crass for your brand, there are other more subtle calls to action you can employ within your content. An effective tactic is to work a question into your content for your followers to respond to in the comments, which often prompts further replies and discussion—all boosting your comment count.

Giveaways are also a great tactic for creating engagement and bringing in new followers. You might want to consider offering your product or service to one lucky winner (whether chosen at random or based on a metric like top-liked comment or post), which will of course cost you the time/materials/labor plus any applicable shipping, etc. However, oftentimes the rules to enter a giveaway on social media will encourage a wave of new engagement in a variety of ways: Some require all entering to follow their account, like the post, comment, tag friends, and sometimes even create posts of their own in the name of the brand. If done right, a giveaway can be extremely impactful (and cost-efficient) publicity that builds up your platform. One disclaimer: Depending on your state or country, giveaways might be considered a form of gaming or be subject to certain regulations, so always check any and all local laws before running a giveaway of your own.

It might take a while to really figure out what your audience responds to and what best fits with your brand, but you will eventually get there through trial-and-error and—most importantly—consistency. Not every post is going to go viral, and some might not even perform that well, and that can be a little disheartening when you're putting yourself out there for the entire world. But every post will capture an audience, and each consistent post will help you get the algorithm on your side. Your aim shouldn't be to go viral, but rather to create a brand and capture the attention of loyal followers who will convert to customers.

Consistency is the key. Some people find setting a social media calendar of scheduled uploads and "shoot days"—where you can batch film content all at once and then post throughout each week at a regular time—is helpful for both personal productivity and hitting the algorithm, but anyone who tries to tell you there is any one "right time" of day or hour for posting is probably incorrect. The truth is that the best timing is hard to nail down and changes constantly, and you'll have to find what works best for you and your particular niche. However, making batches of content to post over time is a great idea, especially if you are busy and managing your business alongside another job/hustle/kids/etc. Some also find that going live immediately after posting on TikTok helps your video get out to more people, bring more people into your livestream, and ultimately gain followers/customers. Again, these are all just general suggestions that you can take and tweak to suit your own personal situation.

If you can post every single day, great. If you can't commit to posting so often, that's okay too. You should strive to post three times a week at minimum, but ultimately it's important to just get online however much you can. Even when you don't have time to make videos or posts to add to your feed, you can still interact with followers by replying to their messages or leaving comments on other videos. The more active you are, the more you will be rewarded by the algorithms with visibility and—most importantly—the closer your followers and customers feel they are to you and your brand. Because the more connected they are to the business, the more orders you will get. That's the end game you should never lose sight of.

There exist a couple tools that can help you batch post your content and make sticking to your social media schedule so much easier. If you can put aside just a couple minutes each week, tools like Loomly and Planoly can help you plan out your entire month with efficiency and ease. These apps can let you essentially "set it and forget it" by scheduling posts, with one exception: Instagram Reels. At the time of this writing, Reels does not allow users to preselect trending audio using these tools, but I hope that the platform will change this in the future.

Once you have spent some time building up your platform and business, you may want to consider collaboration as a way to get your brand out there. Collaborations and brand deals with influencers is the next level of marketing, but it's not guaranteed to bring sales. You really have to do your research and vetting to get the most out of influencer marketing.

There are two types of influencers to consider: macro and micro. Macro-influencers have a minimum of 150,000 followers and usually focus on lifestyle or other broad genres of content.

They often require monetary payment alongside free products, but they will generally lead to actual sales. Exposure on their platform is ultimately a numbers game; the more people who see your brand, the more likely someone is going to buy it.

Micro-influencers are any accounts with less than 150,000 followers. Their fees are typically lower, and they usually want free products. These smaller influencers are great for generating content and raising some small brand awareness; they don't often lead to actual sales.

You should note here that as anyone with an account could be considered a micro-influencer, you'll inevitably have your inbox flooded with so-called "influencers" asking to collaborate for free stuff. If you gave out products to every single person who asked, you would hurt yourself financially for very little, if any, PR benefit. If you respond to these requests at all, you're going to have to get good at saying no and figuring out whether the juice is worth the squeeze.

If someone reaches out with a collaboration offer, check out their platform and have clear and concise expectations of what they should be posting in exchange for what you send. As a personal lesson learned, I once gave a girl with 4,000 followers Elysian perfume only to see her make one post on her story. That was a disappointment that brought no benefit to the brand. Some influencers see themselves as bigger than they really are and may think that their four-figure follower count means that they can provide valuable exposure to brands, but this is just not the case. It's on you to really see who is worthwhile and at what cost.

That's not to say that you should try to work with only the biggest influencers possible. Focusing on the niche will always work better than just general promotion, and it's best to find influencers who are already in it. The best influencers to work with are ones who have built their platform within your product or service because all of their followers are already interested and infinitely more likely to buy. People are already following them for their opinion on this specific thing, and so they carry more sway and credibility when they feature a brand on their platform. These are the collaborations that lead to sales.

Recently, I've figured out a collaboration agreement that works best for me with respect to the price, content, and utilization. I only work with influencers who agree to let me use their content beyond their initial post, including using their content as ads in return for monetary compensation. It's a win-win that also kills two birds with one stone: I get the initial exposure to their followers and content I can repurpose as an ad in perpetuity. This makes paying them well worth it to me, and also better benefits the influencers I work with and allows me to access slightly elevated accounts as well.

A little "industry secret" you may not know is that an influencer's follower count might not even be legitimate. You might be impressed by someone with a million followers, but most of them could have been purchased to artificially pad their numbers and gain exposure. You should always check what other engagement they have to see if it aligns with their purported number of followers. If someone has 100,000 subscribers on YouTube but only a few thousand views per video, or if an Instagram model with 50,000 followers is only bringing in a couple of likes per post, that's a red flag.

However, you should also know that these "influencers" can not only buy followers, but they can buy views, likes, and engagement (i.e., comments) too. Every form of engagement is seemingly for sale on the grimier corners of the internet, but

I always recommend checking their comments because those are less often bought and it's easier to spot fake ones. This of course may change in the age of AI, but at least for now, it's something to check out.

Whether you're reaching out to an influencer or responding to a request for collaboration, you should always ask to see someone's insights before working together if possible. Their insights, like average watch time of videos and other metrics, can help you better determine whether this influencer is legit while a breakdown of their audience's majority gender and age can also indicate if this influencer is reaching your target demographic. More information is always good, so it's certainly worth asking for.

If fielding a bunch of DMs isn't for you, you can streamline your search by utilizing an influencer marketing platform. These platforms help you find the right influencer based on their content type, follower count, and compensation expectations. They further help you manage your collaborations and sometimes even track the reach and effectiveness as well. Some require a subscription to join, but many find the cost well worth it.

Social media may seem like an overwhelming mountain to climb in and of itself, but when utilized correctly it can be one of your greatest assets to promote your business. If you have a little forethought and put in the work, you can make each post, like, and comment work for you.

CHAPTER EIGHT
YOUR NEW BEST FRIEND, AI

What was once just a sci-fi plotline has now become a reality of our daily lives: artificial intelligence. AI has crept its way into automating so many forms of communication, art, and even healthcare. There's no telling what further innovations we may see in coming years, but it's certain that AI is going nowhere anytime soon. You can resist these changes, or you can figure out how to make AI work for you.

We've all seen some major AI fails: too many hands or fingers on an artificial person, incorrect spelling on objects in a picture, and videos that have a weird stiffness that screams auto-generated. While it may bring a good laugh, no business owner is going to want those hiccups in their campaigns. That said, AI is rapidly growing and changing on a daily basis, so those issues are constantly being improved upon. It's an ever-changing landscape constantly featured in our news feeds: self-driving cars, Alexa and Siri, website bots, videos created by AI. There are benefits and drawbacks to society's newfound obsession. It simplifies work, but there are other concerns such as security and the ever decreasing lack of humanity (think how many auto-dialers you receive a day trying to reach you about your car's extended warranty). I'm not here to say you should disregard the benefits of AI and technology based on a few drawbacks. For me, it's all about context. I'm not hailing all AI as good, but I *will* embrace the available technology to improve my approach and practices.

Ask a Bot

If you navigate to most websites, you'll see a prime example of AI in practice. You're often greeted with a bot that offers assistance and the opportunity to ask basic questions. This is standard practice for most pages, but it can be an effective way to offer basic customer service. Many site visitors often navigate to the FAQ page, then ask a bot if they still have questions. AI bots are easy to add to your business page—if you're working with a platform like Shopify, these bots are integrations that you can program to answer and engage with simplified topics like: "Track Order," "Product Question," "Report Issue," etc. AI doesn't replace the personal touch you need for business success, but it can provide customer support in a timely manner and improve overall satisfaction.

Some websites utilize AI chat bots to handle these perfunctory interactions with their customers, and others—like myself—don't. While I had a chat bot enabled on execuluxe.com, I found that it was personally too difficult to manage. Too many times, site visitors would "stump" the bot by asking questions that the AI software could not find the answer to. Many of the questions turned out to be rather basic and easily answered by a human, and the bot only wasted everyone's time. Chatbots can be immensely helpful for answering simple questions, but it's not for everyone, and you shouldn't feel like you have to have it just because it's there.

AI offers a lot of business "hacks," but you still have to do the work. The quality isn't guaranteed, so *you* are responsible for the follow-through. Personally, I use tech tools as a foundation on which to build. When I launched my first batch of perfume, ChatGPT wasn't yet on the horizon. I can distinctly remember agonizing over the best-suited names for different fragrances and the complementary product descriptions—enticing yet informative and evocative prose that allows customers to imagine the scent before they even purchased it. It took me *six hours to write four of these*. I was searching "list of unique words that mean fresh" and struggling with the balance of finding words that embodied my brand while still describing the scent. With ChatGPT in hand, I recently generated nine different fragrance names and accompanying descriptions in just 90 minutes. That's no exaggeration. All I needed was something to organize my thoughts and ChatGPT provided that assistance.

I saved 16.5 hours of time, time I could redirect towards other work for my businesses. AI and ChatGPT aren't a trend that'll fall by the wayside; these are unparalleled tools that will expedite your business while distinguishing you from brands that clutch at the old ways. There is a learning curve, of course. You have to speak the same language as ChatGPT. It needs prompting, and you have to provide a basic description to achieve the desired results. It will sometimes get things wrong, but all you have to do is ask in another way. But even if you have to watch a video on how to use ChatGPT, I can basically guarantee that you'll still save time by using it to complete some of your straightforward tasks.

I've noticed many companies are turning to ChatGPT to help with product descriptions. A tell-tale sign is the overuse of words like "embark" and "allure." I don't know why ChatGPT loves these adjectives so much, but it does.

A Snapshot in Technology

The perfect photo of your products can make or break a sale. Is the lighting right? The angle of the product? Is the photo dynamic or do your eyes pass right over it? There are many considerations and decisions to make, not to mention a myriad of other tasks you need to finish to launch your products. I don't limit myself to just photoshoots or only AI—the best approach for me is a combination of the two. I let AI and technology enhance what I've already accomplished. For me, this combination creates the best results.

I even used the headshot service, tryiton.ai, and uploaded about 10 photos of myself there, and it came back with 100 headshots. Some of them were absolutely terrible, but some were usable and realistic. I still prefer the authenticity of a branded photoshoot with my favorite photographer, but if you're in a pinch and need a professional photo, this service works well. Here's a couple headshots that AI gave me:

Technology didn't just help me with headshots. I use PhotoRoom to create studio-quality product photos on a practical budget. I knew that fragrance bottles would be difficult to pose with and accentuate, so I took a look at the available tech tools to make it happen digitally. Now, I just snap my photo, navigate to PhotoRoom to remove the backgrounds, and tell the AI what I want my perfume bottle to be in front of or next to. The results are uncanny. It can even generate flatlays, which is so great. I recommend anyone with an actual product download Photoroom and use that service. It will enhance your product photos in ways you didn't think were possible.

I take a different approach for my luxury bags though. They're easier to get high-quality product images for, so I don't need to use technology to dress it up. Instead, I work with two different photographers, one in Orlando and the other in LA. I've rented out Peerspaces (think fancy Airbnbs rented by the hour for creative projects or events) and have models go there to pose with my bags. At the same time, I have gathered many friends and associates for photoshoots as well. After all,

I created these bags to meet my needs and the needs of other executives like me, so why not show this in my marketing?

Communication Rollout

Some tasks are so basic that it's not the best use of your time and energy to have an employee (or yourself) complete them. Think of standard correspondence, such as purchase follow-ups, sales and coupons, and more. While these are not technically a result of AI, they are examples of basic technology integration that can make a difference in your day-to-day. I personally use Klaviyo, a well-known platform for "media that connects." Regardless of whether you use Mailchimp, Klaviyo, HubSpot, or one of the numerous other options, I recommend enrolling in an email campaign service. I use several email flows: a "Welcome" flow, a "Browse Abandonment" flow, a "Cart Abandonment" flow, and a "Winback" flow. A "Welcome" flow is an email series, usually five to six emails sent to the customer at intervals (typically a few days apart) to remind them about your company. You may also want to include an offer in this flow, such as a code for 20 percent off their first purchase. The subsequent emails in the flow are to remind them of the discount and to try to capture their attention. A "Browse Abandonment" flow is set up to where it will send your potential customer an email and say something like, "You forgot to check out." It will have the item they were looking at in the email to remind them and may come with a discount code to get them to complete the purchase. The "Cart Abandonment" flow is essentially the same thing but gives them that nudge to complete the purchase with the item they left in their cart. Finally, a "Winback" flow is sent a couple of weeks after they initially went to your website to try and get them back in the shopping flow. This can be sent to both customers who haven't purchased in a while, or customers that never purchased. When paired with text message automations, these emails really help with client orders and retention. Once you set it and forget it, it does all the heavy lifting for you.

 In the same vein, consistent social media engagement can also fall on the AI job description. You can not only use AI to help you come up with posting ideas, but even to post the content for you once you schedule it out. I personally use Loomly for all of my batched content, while Manychat is great for engaging with followers.

Look for the Assist

Technology is the cornerstone of e-commerce as well as many other businesses. Today's reality is that you can't ignore technological advancements if you want to keep pace with competitors. Beyond your website and AI assistant, you should always be on the lookout to incorporate technology features that best suit your needs.

Technology opens the doors to make your business more accessible to buyers and sellers alike. Even so, technology shouldn't replace every step and task, or you'll lose some of the humanity in your brand.

I designed my products—the fragrances and the bags—manually, the "old-fashioned" way, using sample products and materials, though I did receive a digital rendering of the design prior to purchase. My stepdaughter and I worked hard to design the packaging, and we individually wrap each box and send it out—no technology here to speed that up! On the other hand, marketing and finance lie almost entirely in the digital world. Social media and ad campaigns, online banking—it's all technology-based and supported by AIs. With technology at every turn, it's a mistake to overlook the benefits it can bring to your business and to elevating your brand.

Case in point, I was recently browsing the internet and found the Perfumer's Workbook formulation software, sponsored by PerfumersWorld. It's a database for scents, suppliers, formulas, what ingredients work well together, cost of compounds—the resource list of this software is endless. If not for the immense advancements in technology, this program would not exist, and I wouldn't be spending the next month exploring and integrating it into my existing e-commerce business.

Tools like this and AI can also be a game-changer for your businesses' branding strategies and campaigns. And having a great brand is how you get your business to the top of the mountain, so embrace every piece of technology you find to make that trek easier.

CHAPTER NINE

MANAGING THE HUSTLE

Unless you are fortunate enough—or have taken the calculated risk—to be able to focus solely on your business, you will have to manage your startup efforts alongside all other responsibilities. This might mean juggling a full-time job, kids, school, relationships, and everything else that comes with a busy adult life. Part of creating your own business means that you will have to learn to manage the hustle. Sometimes this ultra-packed life is only the reality until you can get the business off the ground; sometimes it's a long-term choice you've made for a multitude of reasons. Though my days are certainly busy running two e-commerce businesses and an agency, I don't see myself leaving insurance anytime soon. As you may know from my debut book *Soul Beneficiary*, I spent years building my client book and investing in my insurance work. Even though Elysian Parfum and Execuluxe® ignite my soul, at this point, I don't plan to ever move away from insurance—it's the industry that made me into an entrepreneur, and I can't imagine a life without it.

Not everyone is so used to handling so many things at once though, so you might experience a bit of a learning curve here. I won't sugarcoat it: Being an entrepreneur is a *lot* of work, and it's not even just the business. But the one thing you're guaranteed in the business world is a master lesson on managing the hustle. To get you started, I'll review a few tools to help you better handle the workload that comes with a new business, in addition to your other responsibilities.

Time Management

If you take nothing else from this chapter, know that the backbone of your success is going to be time management. As the business owner, you have freedom not many are fortunate enough to enjoy—you are your boss—but you also have to provide yourself structure and accountability—you're also your employee. You need to take responsibility for *everything*. That means being mindful of how you use your time and what you spend it on. How you spend the 24 hours each day will ultimately determine the fate of your business.

Without a boss setting expectations and monitoring work, some people struggle with motivation and self-management. The same is often true for work-from-home jobs. If you're operating your new business out of the house, this pressure is doubled. Without the rigors of the office, you may find yourself overtaken by side tasks and constantly distracted. I used to struggle with this during my early days as an insurance agent. You're left cold-calling to build a client book, and it becomes too easy to say, "I'll just watch TV until my laundry is done. And *then* I'll get started." But then I'd finish folding laundry in the middle of a show, and I'd decide to sit through until the end of the episode. Before I knew it, it was time for my kids to get out of school, and I hadn't even made a single call! It's all too easy to get lured away by distractions like this when you're self-employed, especially when you don't have a structure for yourself. Luckily, these pitfalls can be avoided if you set yourself up with the right environment and a clear schedule using something like my Time Block Sheet.

When you feel overwhelmed thinking of everything you need to get done, this sheet helps you break down your day and figure out exactly how to fit every last task into your waking hours. Time blocking is an admittedly boring but extremely necessary part of being self-employed. When I first entered the entrepreneurial lifestyle, I was pretty loosey-goosey with my time and hit on tasks whenever I felt like it. After all, isn't the best part of being your own boss, having that freedom? I quickly learned that this kind of "freedom" can easily keep you from getting work done if you aren't careful. You are your boss, but if you don't act like it, you can become your own worst enemy. Time blocking is the structure you need to stay on track.

Instead of having errands to run, a house to clean, customer emails to respond to, and orders to pack at indeterminate times, time blocking will help you assign a number of hours to each task and schedule them into your day. It's no longer a mess of to-do items floating around your head; it's responding to client emails from 9 a.m. to 9:30 a.m., cleaning the house from 10 a.m. to noon, running errands from 1 p.m. to 3 p.m., packing orders from 3:30 p.m. to 4:30 p.m., making dinner and bonding with the kids, and then communication with overseas designers and manufacturers from 7 p.m. to 9 p.m. Even with breaks included for meals and other miscellaneous tasks, this gives you a *lot* of time to accomplish everything you want to in that day. It makes your whole to-do list possible.

The Time Block Sheet is especially helpful for new entrepreneurs as it forces you to plan out your days and see what you have to get done. These days, I wake up and automatically know what tasks I need to address and at what times I'll complete them. Time blocking is so easy that it becomes ingrained in you over time.

Your "Second Shift"

In the early stages of your startup, you have to think of the work you're doing for the business as your "second shift" of the day. You may have another job or a myriad of other responsibilities going on simultaneously, but you must "clock in" and put in the time and effort if you ever want to see your business succeed. Time blocking is effective for organizing your work and your time, but there are other steps and approaches you can explore in order to make the most of your time.

Something you may benefit from is a dedicated working space, or perhaps a personalized routine to help you transition into your "second shift," working on your business. If you have the space for it, a home office is immensely helpful because it designates a space as a "work area." An office can help remove the visual clutter and distractions of home life and allow you to focus solely on the task at hand. Some people feel a mental shift as soon as they walk through that door and find themselves immensely more productive that way. My basement is solely dedicated to Elysian Parfum and Execuluxe®, and this extra space was a big factor in choosing this house. It gives me the space to create as well as store my products. As soon as I go downstairs, I'm locked in and focused on what I need to accomplish.

If you're living with a little less square footage, you can still create a work corner with a desk in your bedroom or even designate a specific seat at the dining room table as your work spot.

In addition, there are also little routines you can create that will help you make the switch into work mode as smoothly as possible. That could mean taking a brief walk to get your blood flowing and clear your head of other thoughts and responsibilities so you're ready to focus on your startup, or simply lighting a certain candle or turning on a special playlist. This ritual is different for everyone, but eventually, you'll find your "thing" through trial and error and make the most of your time.

The Sacrifice for Success

Not everyone wants to hear this, but it's the truth nonetheless: It's not about whether you *can* do something; it's about how much you *want it* and whether you will make the necessary sacrifices for it. You can accomplish pretty much anything if you are willing to experience a little discomfort or sacrifice. Are you willing to lose a couple hours of sleep, skip socializing with your friends, and fall behind on your favorite show's new season? Yes? Good—that's exactly what it takes to make your business a priority.

Even if you're not living your ideal life right now, it's no small feat to give up the little joys you have in the day in favor of higher productivity and performance. Sometimes watching that one TV show or sleeping in that extra hour can be the highlight of your day, and it may seem unnecessary to sacrifice it. But sometimes, those little pleasures are exactly what keep us from creating a better life for ourselves. It's almost like we become content with discontentment. You need to embrace the discipline to deny yourself these indulgences in order to reach your goals. As I tell people all the time, you have to sacrifice a little bit of the life you have now to get the life you want.

Some people make excuses that they don't have any free time and nothing they could sacrifice to make their dreams happen, but that's almost always untrue. If you look in all the nooks and crannies of your day, you can come up with little pockets of productive time. This may mean strategically cutting back on sleep or maximizing any breaks you may have in the day. Rome wasn't built in a day, and neither will your business be. But that one extra hour in the morning or at night or those 10 free minutes you find here and there will accumulate to make a huge difference. I tell agents all the time that if they could dial for 50 minutes a day, that's approximately 50 dials—which adds up to 18,000 dials a year. That's huge, and it's absolutely attainable when it's broken down like this.

You can also maximize the time you have by learning to multitask. And yes, I know that, scientifically, your brain still has to switch between the tasks, but take a look at a mother holding her baby while cooking dinner while helping her fourth-grader with homework, and tell me that multitasking isn't happening. It's possible to do two things at once, and I can say that I'm a skilled multitasker.

While taking calls, you have the opportunity to catch up on housework, pack orders, cook dinner, or any other mindless task on your to-do list. Some tasks are almost entirely physical, leaving you the opportunity to keep your brain busy through other tasks or by learning new skills and acquiring more knowledge.

We are very blessed to live in a day and age where we can access a university's worth of education at the push of a button. Whether you want to learn how to design your own website, understand the intricacies of a social media rollout and set it up yourself, or find a platform for team communication, you have an abundance of free resources to choose from. You can play audiobooks, podcasts, and videos while doing some other task, thereby maximizing your time. It might not be as immediately gratifying as mindlessly scrolling through TikTok or Instagram in your free time, but you'll come to find it is much more rewarding.

I should add the caveat here that nobody should be working at 100 percent, 24/7, indefinitely. You need to stop and take a break at some point—either by choice or by burning out completely. If you can, I recommend scheduling in one day or even a few hours each week for yourself. Most of the time I end up working all seven days out of the week, but Sunday night is *always* saved for our family dinners. Sunday has historically been the day that I prioritize having family time with my children, and though they aren't kids anymore, Sundays will always be about connecting with them, my husband, stepdaughter, and those closest to me. Work is important, but it's not *the most important thing in life*.

Self-Education vs. Education as Procrastination

In many ways, self-education can be a more powerful tool than formal education. Even reputable institutions are recognizing the value of virtual learning; Harvard offers classes online, as do most accredited colleges. You don't need to buy a book or enroll in a class to learn. You just need to open up Google. It's that easy, and you are only doing a disservice to yourself if you don't take advantage of all the resources at your disposal.

You can never know too much, but you *can* spend too much time trying to learn everything about your business before launching. It's a strange form of subconscious self-sabotage

I've seen time and again. I've had agents who spent months going over the intricacies of every possible plan while never actually picking up the phone. It's months of prep without a single minute spent working. All that knowledge is useless without implementation.

In insurance sales, I always tell agents they are ready after a week of training. They might not know everything, but they have certainly acquired all the fundamentals at this point and are ready to jump on the phone. The sooner they start talking to clients, the sooner they'll start learning how to deal with all the issues and intricacies that come along with insurance. In e-commerce, I use three months as a good rule of thumb to tell when it's time to switch from preparation to action. If you've developed the product or service (which is the hardest part), it should not take you any more than three calendar months to get everything ready and launch your business. Anything more than that, and it's time to take a look and what could be holding you back. Sometimes, the answer is you. Whether it's self-doubt regarding your abilities or fear of failure, you have to get beyond that obstacle and make your business a reality. Entrepreneurship is a continuous education, and you're ready for the challenge.

Of course, this begs the question: How do you know whether you've learned enough to start your business versus whether you're using learning as a procrastination tactic to avoid doing the actual work? Unfortunately, the answer isn't clear-cut. There is no quantitative marker to determine when you're ready. In fact, I don't think you can ever be 100 percent "ready." There are always going to be curveballs, and you'll always have to experience a learning curve. That said, you just need to grasp the fundamentals and the core of your business; you'll learn the rest along the way. But you have to get going. You can acquire a PhD's worth of knowledge all you like but until you put what you've learned into practice, you will not see a single cent.

Even after all these years in the insurance industry, I still don't know everything. But I learn something every day on the job, and you will too. You have to get your business out there and get moving, and in time, you'll find that you learn much more on the job actually doing the work than you ever did simply studying it.

Your 24 Hours

People ask me all the time, "How do you have the time for everything?" They expect superhero tales or a confession about a caffeine addiction. But no, the answer is far less exciting: How would I not have the time? These are my priorities.

We all have the same 24 hours in a day. What defines us is how we use that time. I choose to spend my hours working toward all of my goals and aspirations, e-commerce and insurance alike. It's as simple as that. I want to do the work, and I want to reach these milestones more than I want to do other things. I've somehow managed to combine my interests and hobbies into an actual business—or three. For me, there is nothing more relaxing than making perfume, and I've found a way to make it profitable.

Your actions are informed by your motivations, and motivations come down to your mindset. This is where you find out whether you think like an employee or an entrepreneur. An employee's worst fear is losing their job—a true entrepreneur's worst fear is having to look for one. Me? I don't ever want to go back to working for someone else ever again, and I'm going to do what it takes to keep that from ever happening.

At the end of the day, it's all about what you value and what you're willing to prioritize above other things. When you begin to decide to skip TV before bed and utilize the spare minutes you find in your day, you'll see that there is a lot more time available than you ever imagined. So it's not really about managing a hustle for me; it's about *embracing* the hustle for the sake of my passions.

CHAPTER TEN
NURTURE AN ENDURING CULTURE

According to *Fast Company*, one in five Americans left a job due to poor company culture in 2022.[4] It may not sound significant, but if you have a 100-member team, that's 20 people. Could you afford to lose 20 people? It's far less expensive—and better for morale—to improve your company culture and increase retention.

Culture is one of the most overlooked business fundamentals out there. Entrepreneurs become so focused on the numbers (the sales, inventory, and prospects) that they forget the inner strength needed for a business to succeed. Culture is the way your business operates, from boss to employees, employees to customers, and beyond. If you've ever been a part of a toxic workplace, you know how quickly your feelings towards that job change.

A cutthroat culture is a business killer. You may enjoy the short-term wins that competition breeds. Great, congratulations. But what about the future of your business? Taking success shortcuts without regard to consequences will only breed issues down the road. The other shoe is going to drop eventually, and when it does, you'll find the damage to your brand's reputation, disillusioned and lackluster employees, and falling performance of your company to be a price too great to pay for fleeting success. It's about doing things right, right now, to grow and succeed in the long term.

I'm here to say that you do not have to scam people to succeed. Put the time in to nourish a strong culture, and you'll be rewarded with a strong business. If you can create a company that operates in line with your internal values—one that has a strong, authentic culture—it will pave the way for you to persevere through the entrepreneurial challenges ahead.

Quality Culture

A crucial part of creating an enduring business is establishing an atmosphere favorable for success. The top-quality employees you want working for you will be drawn to your company if you embody a strong, positive company culture. Some of the most important traits include:

- low turnover and opportunity for growth,
- transparent and responsive management,
- recognition of success and achievements, and
- healthy work-life balance among employees.[5]

The correlation between positive company culture and overall success is clear: "Companies with good culture report four times higher revenues," and "Eighty-nine percent of highly engaged employees say the culture in their organization is positive."[6] When the people within your company are happy, they're willing to work so much more than someone who simply shows up and half-asses the work for a paycheck. That one unhappy employee can bring down the morale of the entire team. Now imagine what a whole office full of unhappy employees looks like—it's not pretty, right? A bad culture can cause the death of your business, but it's preventable. All it takes is a little forethought.

What makes for a "good" company culture? Well, it's the same qualities that make for a good job: a supportive workplace, competent and collaborative coworkers, rewarding pay, everything that you would look for in a job yourself. One of the most important elements of a good company culture is a good boss. As the saying goes, "People don't quit a job, they quit a boss." The culture starts with you.

Imagine the ideal job you could have and then determine how you can build it within your company. Of course your vision comes with limits, but you can create policies and structures that promote collective growth while recognizing and rewarding individual success as well.

Even if you're in the early stages of your business, you need to prioritize a business that supports morale and empowers employees. It's the happy, fulfilled employees who will have the motivation to reach new heights, thereby bringing success to your company and elevating your bottom line. Make your business a place where people *want* to work, and you will be rewarded tenfold.

Who's on Your Roster?

Employees are the cornerstone of a successful company. It's the people you work with who determine the company's culture. They are the face of the company and represent it to the world; you want that to be a good impression, right? Having been on the receiving end of some terrible workplaces, I've made culture a key focus of my companies. While I have more 1099 agents than I do W-2 employees, it's still my responsibility to create a positive culture.

At Inspired Insurance Solutions, LLC, I give agents autonomy. They are in full control of their schedules. This may not work for every business out there, but as the COVID pandemic taught us, there's more flexibility with work hours/location than the "standard" way of doing things suggests. Insurance is flexible work, so I applied that same quality to the agent culture. No one should have to choose between holding down a job and picking up their kid from school. If someone needs to leave every day at 2 p.m. to pick up their child, no problem—we make our own schedules, and everyone is remote. It's also commission-only, so you get out what you put in. I want my agents to be happy and productive, and one way to do that is to not breathe down their necks and micromanage everything they do.

I often joke with my agents that I work 18/7, just because I'm always reachable during my waking hours. Even if they don't approach me for answers, my agents are all connected through an app on their phones. It's an established network with people all over the country, which allows them to ask questions and seek advice at any time, regardless of the different time zones. In addition, I have an entire library of resources established to support agents through their training and guide them to close deals. As they build their client books and reach milestones, I offer them rewards for their incredible progress. I want to celebrate that progress because it *is* meaningful. Essentially, I strive to treat each agent as human and to meet them on their level. And it works. While commission-only insurance has an average turnover of 92 percent, my rate is closer to 70 percent.

Many people don't have what it takes to be self-motivated entrepreneurs—you can thank the school system for training people to become employees—so I emphasized a culture of mutual respect and transparency with and among my agents.

You can apply this same mindset with your employees. Listen to their needs. Create open lines of communication. Establish a culture that respects them and supports *their* dreams. Treat your employees right, and they'll stick by your side throughout all stages of growth.

Consider Staci. She was one of my original hires (not an agent but an actual, in-office W-2 employee). I can tell you that, despite my initial and consistent success, there were still roadblocks to building Inspired Insurance Solutions, LLC. But that didn't matter to Staci. She's stuck through every hurdle alongside me, and she has become everything people search for in a good employee—and I have, in turn, ensured she is thoroughly rewarded for that loyalty.

Not everyone is such a diamond in the rough, though. There's the harsh reality of firing in every industry. No one *wants* to fire people—I find it to be the absolute worst part of my entire job. No matter what end you're on, nobody walks away happy in this situation. It's uncomfortable to give that news, and it's devastating to receive it. In a perfect world, firing would never happen.

Nonetheless, I've had to fire people for various reasons. The earliest one was when my first assistant stole my credit card. While that's fireable and illegal, I naively gave her another chance. Yet, throughout the following year, my distrust grew more and more. Eventually, it was clear she didn't care much about the position or me, so I had to let her go.

Attitude is a big part of hiring and firing. I had another employee who had the worst attitude. She would continually bring her personal problems to work. If she was having a bad day, she made the whole team suffer. That dark energy was smothering our culture, so I had to act. Then there was the social media manager who misrepresented himself on his resume. Instead of delivering content, he was outsourcing the tasks I gave him and taking credit for other people's work. I only found out because someone on social media tagged me on a post for violating a contract—turns out, the new hire had made a fake contract to get this outsourced work and then never paid the person for their content. It was utterly shocking and messy—obviously, a good reason for him to be fired. In general, your business should be made stronger by firing the person. While it doesn't make the process easier, you have a culture to protect.

You can give people chances, but there are those who will never change their habits or who, inexplicably, refuse to do what is asked of them. That person is like a sickness—if you have one rotten apple, it can spoil the whole basket. I'm a big energy person, so I refuse to let anyone hang around who will endanger my culture. That's the work of a boss, and you have to be ready to do the work.

> **Hiring Out**
>
> There's a difference between hiring out to expand your business versus hiring out to avoid work you don't feel like doing. As a business owner, you should at least have an idea of how each facet of your business runs, and you will most likely need to fill every role in the beginning. It's only as your business grows and your time is better used elsewhere that you should look to hire someone who can take over some responsibilities.
>
> I know how to do most things with Shopify and Meta ads, but I don't have all day to spend on that. My time is better spent elsewhere. By outsourcing this work, I can focus on building my business and improving products while being guaranteed quality work by an outsourced agency.
>
> You can find talented, independent workers everywhere, but some of my favorite sources include Upwork, Fiver, and 99 Designs (for graphics). Using these sites, you can vet people using their portfolios and reviews. Like many business owners, I've connected with some truly talented people who've helped me with everything from email flows to my logo.

Quality Assurance

No matter where you are in your entrepreneurial journey, your workplace culture has the power to lead you into prosperity or send your numbers spiraling down into bankruptcy. As a leader, it's your job to do this quality assurance check and ensure the company's values are embodied and ingrained in the day-to-day workings of your office.

Lead by example here. No matter how busy I am, it's vital to me that my agents get the support and face-to-face they need. Whether it's through resources, our regular meetings, or an impromptu discussion, I'm here to bring transparency and humanity to Inspired Insurance Solutions, LLC. I have no problem hopping on a Zoom to help someone out, and my e-commerce work is just as precious—I have a brand worth defending there. So I protect these cultures because they are the backbone of company success, client satisfaction, and, just as importantly, employee/agent morale.

CONCLUSION

Waking up in my hotel bed, I was hit with a fresh wave of excitement cut with only a small zap of nerves: *This is really happening.* I swung my feet from the comfort of industrially washed sheets onto the ground to get ready. This was the day I would get to see my brand on the billboards of Times Square and watch my beautiful bags make their Big Apple debut! Every minute mattered, and showtime was coming soon. Drinking a single-brewed cup of coffee as I put on my makeup, I still struggled with the reality of this life-changing moment.

I was debuting at New York Fashion Week.

Execuluxe® was born out of my dreams and determination not very long ago, and now my bags were about to be carried down the runway in one of the world's most iconic fashion events. To see my work displayed on a global stage alongside so many leading couture brands was an honor and achievement on par with writing a bestseller or headlining as a public speaker (both of which I have done and can attest to). Not too long after Execuluxe® made its runway debut, I found out Elysian was nominated by *New You* for Best New Fragrance of 2024—and later won. A major magazine read by millions recognized the brilliance and beauty of what we built, and I couldn't be more honored. *And I made it happen for myself.* Nobody did it for me. There was no fast-forward button. Just endless hours of hard work and more than a spritz of passion. Like all things in life, I couldn't just wait around for someone to hand me what I wanted. So much is possible with hard work, and while I am incredibly blessed—everything I've achieved is entirely achievable for other people: Opportunities are available for those who are willing to grasp them.

I don't care if you're an MBA graduate climbing the corporate world or a single mom waiting tables—if you want it badly enough, you can make it happen. Success has very little to do with luck and everything to do with your motivation, work ethic, and ingenuity.

I was not born into wealth. I was not born with industry connections. I started my insurance career with two small children and a burning drive to succeed—that was it. My upbringing gave me that scrappy kid's resourcefulness and a curious mind; I am always ready to figure things out for myself and hungry to learn more, particularly when it ignites my passion like Elysian Parfum and Execuluxe®. It's this cocktail of qualities that has made me an unstoppable force, not easily discouraged on my way to success.

Tenacity, stamina, courage—everything you need to succeed is already within you. You might not have a business degree or mastery of your field, but you have all the resources you need to gain that knowledge right at your fingertips. It's as simple as perusing the internet.

I say simple, but that does not mean the work is easy. None of this is easy. As the saying goes, "If it was easy, everyone would be doing it," and you don't see someone successfully launching their own business every day. Easy is not part of the equation here whatsoever. You have to be willing to work every single day, especially when you don't want to. Work when you're tired, discouraged, and even when you feel like giving up. Work hard, and you'll work past all the self-doubt and fear holding you back from your best life.

If you've made it to the end of this book, then you're clearly dedicated to putting in the miles to start your own business. Every book you read, every article you devour, and every platform you explore further equip you with the necessary knowledge and skills to conquer your own entrepreneurial journey. It is my sincere hope that you have found applicable tools, camaraderie, and inspiration in these pages. I've said before that I am no "guru" or expert in entrepreneurship, but I've been down this road before, and this book is my guide to you. May you stride into a future of hard work with the same adaptability and passion that fuels my entrepreneurial ventures. I'll see you on the trail.

Continuing Education

If you are really serious about getting your e-commerce business up and going, *please* scan the code below. I offer downloads to help you get your Shopify Store started as well as a comprehensive how-to guide on how to create your email flow. I also have templates for your brand guide and mood board, a complete tech stack checklist, and a list of trusted vendors and partners I use.

GLOSSARY

Advertising: Content created and publicized for the express purpose of promoting your business.

Agency: A company that holistically handles a specific need and provides expertise and services related to it. For a business, this would mostly be related to a marketing agency.

Algorithm: In terms of social media, this is the process by which the platform determines which content is gaining traction and should be boosted to their users' feeds.

Artificial Intelligence (AI): Also referred to as "machine learning," this is a type of technology capable of learning from the internet and/or input given by the user to refine its own instructed output. For our purposes, AI is often used as an "advanced google" to quickly gather information available online and often to produce or enhance copywriting and images for your branding.

Brand: The core ethos of your company, also considered the "why," reason, mission, etc., of why your business exists.

Branding: All visual elements and details used to articulate and convey your brand. "Brand" and "branding" are often confused, and things like your logo may be mistakenly thought of as *the* brand when they are, in fact, simply facets of branding. Your brand will dictate your branding, not the other way around.

Brand Introduction: Also called your "brand launch," this is the coordinated and multifaceted plan to introduce your brand to the general public. It may include the announcement of new social media accounts, an advertising campaign, a new product line, a sale, giveaways, a real-life party, etc. All efforts are made with the purpose of raising awareness of the brand in the public consciousness.

Budget: How much money you have to put either into the business or on any one thing within it.

Budget Allocation: The process of determining how much of your initial investment or what goes back into your business will be spent on what specific sector (i.e., product development, marketing, staff, etc.). How you allocate your budget is fluid and will change depending on your business's needs at any given time.

Collaboration: Here, this refers to the working relationship between an influencer and a brand wherein they feature and promote a product to their followers for free product/services and/or monetary payment.

Company Culture: The values and internal operations within a company, i.e., how things are run and how employees are treated.

Content: Any and all text, pictures, or videos that you post on social media.

Cost of Production: As the term indicates, this refers to how much capital it takes to either manufacture your product or provide your service. This would be the total of any and all materials and labor that went into your product or service, as well as lesser-considered incurred costs like port taxes, shipping, insurance, etc.

E-commerce: The essential definition of e-commerce is the act of buying and selling goods or services online, but this is an umbrella term that encompasses several specific types of businesses. For example, Execuluxe® is technically an e-commerce business because I use the internet to communicate with and arrange orders from my manufacturers in China, but it is a completely unique product that is transported and stored here in Georgia before it is ultimately shipped out to the customer. This is distinct from dropshipping, wherein the product is shipped directly from the manufacturer to the customer, with the entrepreneur acting as a middleman in the sale. Meanwhile, Elysian can also be considered an e-commerce business because, while we make all of our perfume in-house, we are currently a 100 percent online business. This is all to say that e-commerce is a fairly expansive term and includes many different types of businesses.

Elevator Pitch: A quick but detailed summary of your business that can be told in under 60 seconds, or in the time it takes to ascend or descend in an elevator. This term is often used in the fiction and screenwriting world, with the idea that the writer can quickly pitch their story idea to a producer or publisher while they share an elevator ride.

Entrepreneur: Someone with the bravery to start their own business. Entrepreneurs can be found in many different industries and launch various types of ventures, but they all generally share the same sense of creativity, grit, determination, and inspiration to dream of new opportunities for themselves and make them happen.

Ideal Customer: A detailed narrative of the exact person you envision purchasing your product or service. This goes beyond just the typical characteristics and forces; you need to define them on an individual and personal level.

Imposter Syndrome: The feeling that you do not belong in the place you occupy, do not truly possess the skills necessary to succeed, or otherwise don't "deserve" your success. A syndrome generally means a collection of symptoms, and the symptoms that encompass Imposter Syndrome can include insecurity, self-sabotage, anxiety, doubting yourself, and other negative emotions.

Influencer: Someone who has amassed a large following on one or multiple social media platforms.

Investment: What you can put in up front to launch your business. This usually refers to the monetary, but often includes your own time and labor as well as giving up other short-term opportunities in order to focus on your business.

Limited Liability Company (LLC): A type of business structure that you can file under the state you are based in. An LLC comes with many pros and cons, so it's best to talk with an accountant who can best advise how you should organize your business based on your specific situation.

Manufacturer: A company that makes either part of or the finished product, or otherwise provides necessary components for the product that you ultimately sell. Most manufacturers have factories and provide the necessary equipment, raw materials, and labor to create your product and, especially in e-commerce, and are often located in China.

Marketing: The coordinated strategies to communicate your brand to the general public, not to be confused with advertising (although the two are closely related).

Market Research: The process of gathering information and data to understand key aspects of your business such as the supply and demand of your product or service at the local or general level, target demographic, related industries, competitors, etc.

Media Kit: An organized, ready-to-go collection of documents provided to members of the media so they can easily gather information for articles, videos, or other publications about the company. A media kit helps you better control the narrative of your business and more likely see a final piece that is "on brand" with the information, phrasing, and visual elements you have provided.

Micro-influencer: An influencer who has a small but not unnotable following. These influencers might be just starting their careers and have the potential to grow much larger over time, or they may have developed their following in a niche area and thus have a more loyal following who may be more effective to promote to.

Net Income: What your company makes after subtracting manufacturing costs, taxes, and other expenses.

Organ: A fixture that perfume makers use to organize and store their many scent notes. It resembles the musical instrument.

Pain Point: A problem or unfulfilled need that the customer has. This can be something as simple as "I want a unique scent to make me feel luxurious" to something emotional and heavy like "I want to ensure that my family is taken care of when I pass away from my terminal illness." In sales, you need to listen for a customer's pain point and then find the right product or service your business provides to address their pain point.

Press Release: A short summary of a press-worthy event within your business (brand launch, new product, milestone reached, etc.) that is written and formatted like an article. A press release can often serve as a basis for a more detailed article written by a publication or be published as-is.

Principles of Sales: A term I created to describe the basic values you should practice when speaking with a potential client or customer. Very simply put, it refers to treating the other person like a human being.

Profit Margin: The difference between the sale price and the cost of production. You want to strive for a product or service that has a high profit margin either by lowering the cost of production or raising the sale price, although either tactic has to be done skillfully so as not to inadvertently reduce your overall quality or price yourself out of the market.

Return on Ad Spending (ROAS): How much you get back in sales for what you put into advertising. For example, if each month you are making $5,000 in sales and spending $1,000 in advertising, then your ROAS is 5x. You should strive for a ROAS of 4x and higher.

Revenue: Also referred to as the gross income, this is the total amount in sales that the business receives.

Sales Script: A general flow of conversation between you and your prospective customer with the goal of selling your product or service to help them fill a certain need.

"Second Shift": This refers to the grind of coming home from work or finishing other responsibilities, only to turn around and immediately start working on your business rather than relaxing. Many entrepreneurs have to work this second shift until they get their business off the ground or otherwise can fully focus on their business.

Social Media Schedule: A planned projection of your posts in the next week, month, year, etc. This schedule helps you predetermine your content and post it on a regular basis, which greatly helps with visibility and growth on the platform.

Target Demographic: The group of people to whom your product or service is most marketable and who are the most likely to purchase from your company. Characteristics of this target demographic may be based on hard data points (such as gender, race, location, income, etc.) or more general (like hobbies, interests, or lifestyles).

Viral Product: A product that becomes well-known through social media.

REFERENCES

1. Arlin Cuncic, "Is Imposter Syndrome Holding You Back from Living Your Best Life?," updated September 23, 2024, https://www.verywellmind.com/imposter-syndrome-and-social-anxiety-disorder-4156469.
2. Jill Morton, "Why Color Matters," Colorcom, accessed October 23, 2024, https://www.colorcom.com/research/why-color-matters.
3. "How to Choose the Right Color Palette for Your Brand," IDG Advertising, accessed October 23, 2024, https://idgadvertising.com/how-to-choose-the-right-color-palette-for-your-brand/.
4. Al Dea, "How to Spark a Revolution in Company Culture That'll Boost Employee Retention," *Fast Company*, March 6, 2023, https://www.fastcompany.com/90849584/how-spark-revolution-company-culture-boost-employee-retention.
5. Eric Tolic, "What Makes a Great Company Culture (and Why It Matters)," *Entrepreneur*, June 8, 2022, https://www.entrepreneur.com/growing-a-business/what-makes-a-great-company-culture-and-why-it-matters/427347.
6. Hristina Nikolovska, "16+ Key Company Culture Statistics for 2024," *Moneyzine*, January 8, 2024, https://moneyzine.com/careers/company-culture-statistics/.

RECOMMENDED RESOURCES

For self-education:
- Google Career Certificates are a low-cost option to learn new skills and become certified.
- Grow with Google offers free skill-building courses, but does not lead to certifications.
- YouTube has literally millions of free videos on every topic under the sun, and you can easily find detailed how-tos, interviews, lectures, etc., on whatever it is you want to learn. Keep in mind that, especially within the entrepreneurial space, many creators put their best videos behind a paywall, but you should still be able to find plenty for free.
- Platforms like Spotify, iTunes, and other audio streaming services host many excellent podcasts for free, especially podcasts on business and entrepreneurship.

For branding:
- Canva is a very user-friendly website that even the most novice can use to create logos, digital banners, posters, etc.
- 99designs can help you find graphic designers by either searching for someone who matches your

envisioned style or running your own contest wherein numerous designers submit mockups based on your specifications and compete for the contract.
- Freelance platforms like Upwork and Fiverr are great resources that let you find an expert to do anything from logo design to building a website.
- While many people don't think about this too much, packaging is a big part of branding, especially for online-only businesses. You should give some thought to the boxes, labels, tissue paper, and tape you use to pack and ship your products off to customers. You can also include postcards, stickers, and other little branded "freebies" with each order to further promote your business and build brand loyalty. For this type of customized printed material, VistaPrint is most popular and often offers sales and discounts, but I find their quality to be lacking on certain products, so I prefer places like Uprinting and Noissue.

For social media:
- The top social media platforms that you should consider establishing a following on include TikTok, Instagram, Facebook, YouTube, Pinterest, X (formerly known as Twitter), Tumblr, and Reddit. There may be some more niche platforms that, depending on your target demographic, you might also want to consider using, but the ones I've listed here are known and used by the vast majority of the general public.
- CapCut is a video editing app that offers templates to automatically edit your video. This app is primarily used for TikTok videos but can also be used to create Instagram Reels and other videos.

- Once again, Canva has a free template to make formatted Instagram slides for posts, and you can also use their other templates to create aesthetic-friendly text posts for other platforms.
- Social Cat is a service that will help you find influencers to collaborate with for brand deals/promotional content. There are many other similar services that you can find by googling something like "influencer marketing," but Social Cat is the one I can personally recommend.
- Loomly is a social media management service that helps you plan out your content in a social media schedule, provides content ideas, automates posts, tracks data, and analyzes each post's impact to accelerate your growth and maximize your reach.

For advertising:
- Meta ads allow you to advertise directly onto the feeds of users on platforms like Facebook and Instagram, targeting your specific demographic.
- Google AdWords is a more exclusive service in that you have to "win" your keywords, and the cost depends on the quality and relevance of your brand, but it is a highly effective way to dominate the search results for products and services related to your business.
- TikTok ads can also be beneficial, and with the added feature of TikTok Shop now available, you can kill two birds with one stone by promoting both your content to grow your following *and* the actual product with a TikTok Shop link.

For websites, online shops, and other digital branding:

- It is super important to own your domain, and services like GoDaddy can help you easily purchase them. If not already claimed or previously purchased, you should be able to get your domain for fairly cheap—some people can claim theirs for as low as $10 a year. If you want to claim a domain that is already owned by someone else or want to claim a high-value domain (which tend to be shorter, use popular words, and relate to big industries, etc.), you can attempt to broker or go through other services to get it.

- GoDaddy, Squarespace, and Wix tend to be the most popular services for user-friendly website building, especially for those who do not have experience. Each one comes with a recurring host fee, and you might need to upgrade to a more expensive plan in order to enable commerce, chat functions, etc.

- To raise visibility and get more business, you have to focus on website and search engine optimization. You can look at freelance sites like Upwork or Fiverr for individual experts, or you can look at services that pop up on the front page when you search "website optimization" (clearly, they must be doing something right).

- Shopify may be known mostly as a dropshipping platform, but it is helpful for *any* e-commerce business because it makes enabling commerce on your website so much easier. You can also use Shopify for other aspects, such as sourcing products if you are dropshipping and building your website.

- Services like Attentive, Klavyio, Manychat, and Postscript can help you automatically send out SMS messages and emails to customers who have already signed up for notifications from your business, which can help alert customers to sales and new drops, encouraging sales.

For product photography:
- Amazon can help you get reasonably-priced equipment to get you set up for photoshoots. A newer-model phone may very well have all the quality you need for photos, but a camera can help elevate the overall quality of your images. For related accessories, you should look to get the following: lighting (I highly recommend a Lume Cube), a stand, a backdrop (sometimes even getting a piece of tile or fabric will suffice), a ring light, and a few product-related props to give depth to your image and align with your branding.
- For nice brand-aligned spaces to hold full photoshoots, platforms like Peerspace allow you to rent locations by the hour.
- Photoroom is an app that utilizes AI to edit and refine pictures by giving them a new background, adding things in, changing the lighting, etc. Especially for those taking photos on their phone, this app really helps elevate the final result and bring it to a professional level.

For sourcing:
- If you are looking to connect with a manufacturer to create a new product, Pietra is a good platform that can help you find sources. ImportYeti can also assist

you in locating manufacturers and suppliers, allowing you to streamline your product development process.
- Wholesale sites like Alibaba allow you to purchase either full products or components at a massive discount compared to retail, but there are often minimum order quantities, shipping costs, and import taxes to consider.

ACKNOWLEDGMENTS

Writing *A Spritz of Sales* has been an incredible journey, and there are so many people who have walked this path with me—lifting me up and sharing their wisdom, energy, and belief.

To my family—thank you for your unconditional love and encouragement. You've been my rock and my sounding board, and I wouldn't be here without your support.

To my mentors, colleagues, and friends—your insights and advice have been invaluable. Thank you for challenging me, guiding me, and always pushing me to think bigger, dream bolder, and work harder.

To the entrepreneurs who inspired this book and whose stories of resilience and determination continue to motivate me—this book is a reflection of the courage, passion, and tenacity we all share.

And finally, to my readers—whether you're just beginning your entrepreneurial journey or are well into your hustle, thank you for allowing me to be a part of your path. I hope this book offers you the tools, encouragement, and inspiration to keep pursuing your dreams.

With gratitude and excitement for all that's to come,
Jessi Park

ABOUT THE AUTHOR

Jessi Park is an author, perfumer, designer, artist, and driven entrepreneur with a vision. She is the founder and president of three companies: Inspired Insurance Solutions, LLC, an A+ BBB top-rated nationwide brokerage that assists thousands of clients in navigating the complex worlds of health, life, medicare, and annuities; Elysian Parfum, a boutique online perfumer crowned Best New Fragrance of 2024 by *New You*; and Execuluxe®, a vegan functional fashion line that debuted at New York Fashion Week 2023 and has continued to overturn the bag market.

Jessi holds a bachelor's degree in communication and business from the University of Central Florida, but some of her most critical education came from overcoming adversity while working her way out of poverty. As a self-made woman, she is passionate about learning to do new and different things on her own and teaching others how to empower themselves to do the same. Among her many other ventures, she is the bestselling author of *Soul Beneficiary*, an internationally collected artist, world traveler, and mother of two adult children and one stepdaughter.

She lives in Georgia with her husband and furry companions.

www.ingramcontent.com/pod-product-compliance
Lightning Source LLC
Chambersburg PA
CBHW070952180426
43194CB00042B/2356